# THE IMPORTANCE OF

# Mother Jones

These and other titles are included in The Importance
Of biography series:

# THE IMPORTANCE OF

# Mother Jones

by
Madelyn Horton

Lucent Books, P.O. Box 289011, San Diego, CA 92198-9011

**Dedication**

*In memory of my brother Michael, another brave fighter.*

Library of Congress Cataloging-in-Publication Data

Horton, Madelyn, 1962–
    The importance of Mother Jones / by Madelyn Horton.
        p.  cm.—(The Importance of)
    Includes bibliographical references and index.
    Summary: A biography of the determined labor
organizer of the early twentieth century who became known
as Mother Jones.
    ISBN 1-56006-057-3  (lib. bdg. : alk. paper)
    1. Jones, Mother, 1843?–1930—Juvenile literature.
2. Women in the labor movement—United States—
Biography—Juvenile literature.   3. Women social
reformers—United States—Biography—Juvenile literature.
4. Trade-unions—Coal miners—Organizing—United States—
History—Juvenile literature.   5. Children—Employment—
United States—History—Juvenile literature.    [1. Jones,
Mother, 1843?–1930.   2. Labor leaders.]    I. Title.
HD8073.J6H67      1996
331.88'092—dc20                                 95-2860
[B]                                      CIP
                                                     AC

Copyright 1996 by Lucent Books, Inc., P.O. Box 289011,
San Diego, California, 92198-9011

Printed in the U.S.A.

# Contents

# Foreword

THE IMPORTANCE OF biography series deals with individuals who have made a unique contribution to history. The editors of the series have deliberately chosen to cast a wide net and include people from all fields of endeavor. Individuals from politics, music, art, literature, philosophy, science, sports, and religion are all represented. In addition, the editors did not restrict the series to individuals whose accomplishments have helped change the course of history. Of necessity, this criterion would have eliminated many whose contribution was great, though limited. Charles Darwin, for example, was responsible for radically altering the scientific view of the natural history of the world. His achievements continue to impact the study of science today. Others, such as Chief Joseph of the Nez Percé, played a pivotal role in the history of their own people. While Joseph's influence does not extend much beyond the Nez Percé, his nonviolent resistance to white expansion and his continuing role in protecting his tribe and his homeland remain an inspiration to all.

These biographies are more than factual chronicles. Each volume attempts to emphasize an individual's contributions both in his or her own time and for posterity. For example, the voyages of Christopher Columbus opened the way to European colonization of the New World. Unquestionably, his encounter with the New World brought monumental changes to both Europe and the Americas in his day. Today, however, the broader impact of Columbus's voyages is being critically scrutinized. *Christopher Columbus,* as well as every biography in The Importance Of series, includes and evaluates the most recent scholarship available on each subject.

Each author includes a wide variety of primary and secondary source quotations to document and substantiate his or her work. All quotes are footnoted to show readers exactly how and where biographers derive their information, as well as provide stepping stones to further research. These quotations enliven the text by giving readers eyewitness views of the life and times of each individual covered in The Importance Of series.

Finally, each volume is enhanced by photographs, bibliographies, chronologies, and comprehensive indexes. For both the casual reader and the student engaged in research, The Importance Of biographies will be a fascinating adventure into the lives of people who have helped shape humanity's past and present, and who will continue to shape its future.

# Important Dates in the Life of Mother Jones

**1837**
Probable year of Mary Harris's birth in Cork, Ireland, though many sources accept 1830, as reported by Mother Jones.

**1840s**
Travels with her mother and two brothers to the United States to join her father. The family settles in Toronto, Canada.

**1858–59**
Attends Toronto Normal School.

**1859–60**
Teaches elementary school in Monroe, Michigan.

**1860–61**
Moves to Chicago, Illinois, and runs a dressmaking business.

**1861**
Moves to Memphis, Tennessee, to teach school again. Meets and marries George Jones, an iron molder and union organizer.

**1867**
Husband and children die of yellow fever in Memphis epidemic. Mary Harris Jones returns to Chicago to resume dressmaking.

**1871**
Loses her shop and all possessions in the Great Chicago Fire. Begins working with the Knights of Labor.

**1877**
Involved in the Great Upheaval railroad strike in northeastern United States.

**1885–87**
Works in Chicago for Knights of Labor. Haymarket Square incident.

**1894**
Is active in Chicago and Birmingham, Alabama, assisting striking coal miners. Works in cotton mills and observes appalling working conditions of child laborers.

**1895**
Helps start the *Appeal to Reason,* a weekly socialist newspaper. Travels, sells subscriptions.

**1897**
Organizes striking coal miners in West Virginia and Pennsylvania.

**1899–1900**
Joins strikers in Arnot, Pennsylvania. Leads "mop and broom brigade march" of miners' wives. Victory celebration at Blossburg.

**1900–1903**
Hired as an organizer by United Mine Workers of America. Works throughout Northeast organizing miners, silk weavers, factory workers. Article "Civilization in Southern Mills" is published in the *International Socialist Review*. Is arrested and jailed for first time while organizing miners in West Virginia.

**1903**
Leads the march of the mill children.

**1905**
Helps found the Industrial Workers of the World (IWW) in Chicago.

**1907–11**
Helps raise money for defense of Mexican revolutionaries. Visits Mexico.

**1912–13**
Arrested and jailed in West Virginia for Paint Creek–Cabin Creek strike, but released on public demand.

**1913–14**
Goes to Colorado to assist striking miners. Meets with governor, leads demonstration in Denver. Repeatedly arrested and jailed. Ludlow Massacre period.

**1915**
Testifies before Commission on Industrial Relations. Visits Rockefeller with UMW representatives.

**1916–20**
Works with striking coal miners in West Virginia. Supports major steel strike in Pennsylvania. Arrested at Homestead.

**1921**
Is honored in Mexico City at Pan-American Labor Congress.

**1922–30**
Retires to Washington, D.C. Eventually moves to farmhouse in Maryland.

**1924**
Writes her autobiography in Chicago. Aids dressmakers on strike.

**1930**
Celebrates one hundredth birthday on May 1. Dies in Hyattsville, Maryland, on November 30. Buried in Union Miners' Cemetery in Illinois.

# Fighting Like Hell for the Living

Mary "Mother" Jones was one of the most successful labor leaders of the early twentieth century. A courageous, high-spirited woman, she spent the greater part of her unusually long life fighting for the rights of working people. Her victories are now so woven into the fabric of working life that they seem commonplace; indeed, they are often overlooked or taken for granted today. But winning them required enormous effort and persistence. Because of labor movement pioneers like Mother Jones, American workers are now guaranteed working conditions they only dreamed of a century ago.

## A Growing Nation

In the nineteenth century, when America was a young, growing nation whose industries were just beginning to produce goods, workers had few rights. The government, wanting to encourage economic growth, set no restrictions on how industries were to be run, nor did it establish requirements designed to protect employees' health or safety. Private companies were unregulated, free to set the standards in their own factories and mines.

Unfortunately, given this latitude, many companies brutally exploited their workers. Employees who suffered injury or illness on the job, a common occurrence in the often hazardous factories and coal mines, could simply be fired and replaced with new hires from the masses of people competing for jobs in the Industrial Revolution. Countless workplaces posed life-threatening dangers. Wages were low and benefits such as sick pay, vacation time, or health insurance were unheard-of. No laws forbade children to work, so thousands spent their earliest years working alongside their parents, who were not paid enough to cover the bills on their own. Employees were expected to work ten to fifteen hours a day, six days a week. In some industries the company's control extended even to the workers' living conditions. Many coal miners, for example, lived in "company towns," near remote mining areas. They stayed in company-owned houses, little better than shacks, whose dirt floors and tar-paper roofs were completely inadequate to the harsh, snowy winters of mountainous coal-mining country. They were forced to shop in company-owned stores, where food and goods were invariably overpriced.

In the absence of unions, workers who complained about the degrading

*Before Mother Jones's crusade for labor reform, nothing prevented companies from hiring children to work long hours in unsafe conditions.*

conditions under which they worked and lived could be, and usually were, fired from their jobs. Consequently, many people toiled away their days in dire poverty, afraid to speak out and feeling helpless about the circumstances of their lives.

The American labor movement that emerged in the mid-nineteenth century gave voice to their distress. Despite great obstacles and opposition, workers began to organize to protest unfair practices. Early union activists, brave pioneers who ignored armed company guards' threats of violence, went deep into company territory, holding meetings in secret to persuade workers to unionize. They planned strategies that would help workers empower themselves and fight for freedom from hardship and oppression.

## A Brave Fighter

Mother Jones, herself a member of the working class, was one of these early pioneers. After suffering substantial hardship and personal tragedy, she resolved to devote her life to helping working people. Called the "patron saint of the picket lines"[1] by one magazine writer, Mother Jones was fiercely loyal to her cause. She had a single-mindedness and a sense of purpose uncommon in its intensity. But in spite of a reputation for toughness, Mother Jones was disarmingly sweet and gentle looking, almost grandmotherly in appearance. She favored Victorian dresses trimmed with lace and often wore fresh violets tucked into the bonnet on her head. Reporters covering her speeches seemed always to comment on her snow white hair, her twinkling, bright blue eyes, and her petite, five-foot size. But though she may have looked fragile and dainty, when she opened her mouth there was no doubt about her strength. "When she rose to speak," a journalist wrote, "Mother Jones seemed to explode in all directions and suddenly everyone sat up alert and listened."[2]

In the days when only the railroad linked far-flung American cities and towns, Mother Jones boarded countless trains and traveled endless miles, organizing and campaigning tirelessly for workers all over the country—her "boys," as she liked to call them. In an age when women were not allowed to join what few unions existed, nor even to vote, Mother Jones exercised a

*Despite Mother Jones's gentle appearance, she was a fierce fighter for the rights of working people.*

powerful influence on her contemporaries. The working people whose rights she fought for loved her. Company owners, millionaire industrialists, and scores of politicians hated and feared her because she stirred men and women to action with her fiery speeches. Her opponents did not know how to contend with the fearless and unflappable white-haired old woman. They tried again and again to stop her from speaking in public. She was denounced on the floor of the U.S. Congress, called "the most dangerous woman in America,"[3] threatened with violence, several times even thrown in jail.

## Strong and Determined

But neither threats at gunpoint nor long nights in jail could interfere with Mother Jones's determination to free the workers; nor could her own advancing age. She did not begin labor organizing until her fifties, and she was still working hard well into her eighties. She even made a trip to West Virginia in her nineties to help coal miners through yet another struggle.

As do most accomplished people, Mother Jones inspired a number of critics and detractors in her long and productive life. Some were shocked by her bluntness and candor and the language that she used, which was often rough and sprinkled with profanities. She was called stubborn.

She was criticized for her determination, her single-mindedness, her refusal to concede an inch on any principle she held dear. And yet, these were the very qualities that enabled her to accomplish the significant things that she did. Mother Jones simply refused to give up, and she did not care what others might think.

In her autobiography Mother Jones reminisced about an incident that had taken place many years earlier. She had been asked to speak at a union meeting in a small West Virginia mining town. When she arrived, she found the miners gathered in a church. The president of the local union was seated at a table in front, and a priest was collecting money. By her own account, Mother Jones marched down the aisle to the front of the church. "What's going on?" she demanded to know. "We rented the church for our meetings," the surprised president replied. "Boys," Mother Jones said, turning to face the miners seated in the pews, her anger rising, "this is a praying institution. You should not commercialize it. Get up, every one of you, and go out into the open fields." When she had reassembled the men in a field outside the church she spoke to them again. "Your organization is not a praying institution. It's a fighting institution," Mother Jones told the miners. "Pray for the dead, and fight like hell for the living!"[4]

They were feisty words, and brave, and entirely typical of Mother Jones. They were the words she lived by.

## Chapter

# 1 "I Was Born in Revolution"

I was born in revolution.

—Mother Jones,
*The Autobiography of Mother Jones*

The day Mother Jones turned one hundred years old—May 1, 1930—the Maryland countryside was bursting with spring. Hundreds of visitors traveled down sunny back roads to the old, out-of-the-way farmhouse where she was staying, bringing fresh flowers and birthday gifts. A steady stream of politicians and labor leaders joined them from nearby Washington,

D.C. The American Federation of Labor had been planning celebrations in Mother Jones's honor in cities around the country. On the appointed day, people gathered in public places in Seattle, Chicago, and New York to hear speeches of praise, eat picnic lunches, and listen to Mother Jones address them over a simultaneous radio broadcast.

She had been living at the Maryland farmhouse, the home of her friends Walter Burgess, a retired miner, and his wife, Lillie May, all through the previous year.

*Mother Jones at her one-hundredth-birthday celebration. Hundreds of visitors gathered in the Maryland countryside to honor Jones, while people across the country listened to the famous labor leader give a radio speech.*

Rheumatism and failing health had kept her bedridden for much of that time, but on the day of her birthday celebration Mother Jones was lively, high-spirited, and bright. "Hell, I've never worn one of these things in my life!" she protested when someone pinned a sweet pea corsage on her dress. She rested in the shade of the Burgesses' apple trees as friends placed an enormous five-layer cake before her, topped with a hundred candles.

Reporters and photographers documented the historic occasion. Having seen only one "talkie" in her life, Mother Jones was thrilled by the motion picture cameras. While Paramount News filmed her, she talked about the need for American workers to "stick together and be loyal to one another."[5] By radio, she spoke to the crowds gathered in distant cities in her honor. She read aloud the telegrams that had poured in from around the world from labor leaders, politicians, and admirers, including one from John D. Rockefeller Jr., a man for whom Mother Jones had sharp words in the past. His message of "heartiest congratulations" delighted her. She regaled her guests with stories about her long years of service to the labor movement and her many escapades.

"I've seen and done just about everything," Mother Jones told one reporter. "In my time electricity replaced kerosene, the automobile took the place of the horse. I've seen the coming of the telephone, radio and the airplane. When I came to America in 1840, Martin Van Buren was President. I lived through the Civil War, the War with Spain and the 1914–1918 War. I've seen the railroads cross the Continent. And, I've been in a thousand battles fought by my class, the working class, against the bosses. I'm a hundred years old, my lad, and I can tell you that I'm very tired."[6]

There is some question as to whether Mother Jones was actually turning one hundred years old that day. Few facts about her early life, including her birth date, are certain. She was already in her fifties when she began organizing workers and making news headlines; before that, reporters had paid her no attention. Records documenting her early life, such as a birth certificate or public school records, are scarce. The only information available about her younger self comes directly from Mother Jones and what she either could recall or chose to reveal. About her personal life, unfortunately, she chose to reveal very little. In her autobiography, she described the entire first half of her life in a few dismissive paragraphs.

As to her age, some historians argue, with evidence, that Mother Jones exaggerated it for effect, or that her memory for dates had grown fuzzy by the time she wrote her autobiography. Either way, she was probably several years younger than she claimed to be on that final birthday. One of her biographers found a baptismal notice in Cork, Ireland, parish records dated 1837, which would have made her ninety-three, not one hundred, on her final birthday. Still, perhaps out of respect for Mother Jones, many sources continue to cite May 1, 1830, as her birth date, and she is widely regarded to have been a centenarian.

## Born in Ireland

Disputes about her birth date notwithstanding, there is little disagreement that

*Irish peasants, evicted from their homes for failing to pay their rent, fill the streets. Frustrated and poor, many of the Irish began to join the rebellion against British rule.*

Mother Jones lived an unusually full and productive life. The first child of Richard and Mary Harris, she was born in County Cork, Ireland, and christened Mary Harris. Two boys soon followed. Mary and her younger brothers spent their earliest years in a humble, one-room cottage fashioned of mud and straw, without windows or running water.

As did many poor Irish peasants, the Harrises rented their roughhewn house from a British landlord. The British government ruled all of Ireland at the time, having conquered the country and confiscated its farmland centuries earlier. Landless Irish peasants had to depend for their livelihood on wealthy British landowners, typically Protestant, who hired Irish Catholic peasants to live on their property and work the land. The peasants used their small wages to pay rent, and for food

they grew what crops they could—usually potatoes—on small patches of land loaned them by the landlords. For generations, the Harris family had been poor tenant farmers in this system.

At the time of Mary's birth, Ireland was in great turmoil. The potato crops, Ireland's diet staple, began to fail and famine swept the land. Seeking income to replace the failed crops, British landlords were raising rents higher than the peasants could afford to pay or turning already scarce farmland into grazing land for their cattle herds. When they could no longer pay rent, hundreds of thousands of peasants across Ireland were evicted. Homeless, with no food and no land on which to grow food, unable to turn to the government for help, hungry peasants filled Ireland's streets and towns, begging for assistance. Trouble loomed.

*An artist's depiction of Mary's hometown of County Cork, Ireland, during prosperous times. At the time of Mary's birth, however, Ireland was experiencing political and economic turmoil.*

The Irish, subjected to centuries of religious, political, and economic oppression at the hands of the British, had been rebelling against British rule for some time, but in the desperate years of the 1830s and 1840s, peasant rebellion against the upper-class landowners took on a new urgency. Secret groups were formed to fight back. These organized resistance groups often resorted to violence, attacking the British and destroying their property. The number of fires, assaults, and murders rose across Ireland as the peasants lashed out against the injustices they had suffered. The violence grew steadily.

Though Mary's family managed to pay their rent, they were among Ireland's frustrated and desperate poor. Mary's father and grandfather began to participate in the general rebellion, meeting with groups of rebels who assembled at night, disguised themselves with blankets or dark clothing, and roamed the streets and towns. Under cover of darkness, the rebels attacked and beat rent collectors and landlords and set fire to their farms and houses. They freed fellow peasants being held as prisoners by the British, and stole food for the hungry.

The British government reacted quickly to suppress these revolutionary uprisings. Soldiers were sent to occupy Ireland and to search the countryside for the rebel peasants. The British soldiers stayed for years, arresting and punishing anyone even suspected of involvement with the secret groups. The punishments were harsh. When Mary was two years old, her grandfather was arrested and hanged by the British. When she was five, a notice was sent out announcing that her father was to be captured and sentenced likewise. British soldiers came to the Harris home in the dead of night, terrifying the small girl and her mother, scouring the house and tearing apart the chimney in an exhaustive research for her father. But they did not succeed. He was already on his way to America.

## A New Life

Richard Harris spent the next five years in the United States working as a laborer. While many of his fellow workers squandered their hard-earned money on alcohol each payday, Mary's father worked hard and saved diligently. When he finally had enough money, he sent for his family.

After a rigorous three-thousand-mile, seven-week journey across the Atlantic Ocean on a cargo ship, the children and their mother, like hundreds of thousands of other immigrants, landed in bustling New York City. Mary was ten years old. Her father settled the family in Toronto, Canada, where he had a job working on the railroad. There, Mary spent the rest of her childhood. Toronto offered free public education, so she was able to attend school. A good student and a hard worker, she was the first Harris to graduate from high school. With her parents' encouragement, Mary then attended a year of normal school, a training school for teachers.

Records do not indicate whether Mary actually completed her normal school training, but even if she had not she still would have been considered well educated for her day and probably would have had no difficulty finding teaching positions. The details of Mary's life during the next several years are uncertain. She may have taken a teaching job in Maine.

### Not a Centenarian?

*In his book* The Speeches and Writings of Mother Jones, *labor scholar Edward M. Steel has written on the confusion surrounding Jones's birth date and her earliest years.*

"It is almost certain that Mother Jones was not born in 1830, and it is unlikely that 1 May was her birthday. However, she had been using those dates for many years, and since she herself was the source of virtually all information about the first 60 years of her life, no one questioned them. The little documentary evidence that exists confirms her general statements about her life, but not specific dates; whole decades lack any support other than her assertions."

*Hundreds of thousands of Irish immigrants sailed to the United States in the nineteenth century with hopes of finding a better life. Here, an Irish family, with all of their belongings in tow, arrives in New York City.*

Records indicate she held a teaching position at St. Mary's, a convent school in Michigan, but left there after only one year. She moved to Chicago and worked as a dressmaker, a skill she had learned from her mother. In the summer of 1861 she moved to Memphis, Tennessee, to try teaching again. There, in the fall, she met George Jones, and they were married two months later.

A Tennessee native, Mary's husband was an iron molder. Molders were highly skilled workers who spent long hours in the hot furnaces of the foundry, melting iron and pouring it into molds. The ironware they made included horseshoes, tools, and tracks for the rapidly growing railroad industry. Dedicated to his trade, George worked hard for ten and twelve hours a day in a scorchingly hot shop. He was a member of one of the few unions in existence at the time, the Iron Molders Union. The union wanted better conditions for the workers and lobbied for higher pay, safety standards, and ventilation for the stifling shops. Few molders

were even aware the union existed, so George spoke about it often to his coworkers and urged them to join.

Bright, self-educated, and conscientious, George made a good match for Mary. He was passionate about the rights of workers, and his convictions undoubtedly had an influence on Mary. The couple settled happily into a small rented house on the outskirts of Memphis, and within two years Mary had given birth to their first child.

## Memphis in the 1860s

In the year before Mary and George Jones were married, civil war had broken out between the North and South in the United States. Tennessee had joined the Confederacy and many residents rallied behind the Southern forces, but George and Mary opposed slavery and secretly hoped the North would win the war. When the Yankees captured Memphis in 1862, the town became an important strategic center for the Union war effort—its location on the Mississippi River and its network of railroads made Memphis an ideal center for transporting Northern troops and supplies. All the increased business caused the interlinked railroad and coal industries to thrive. The iron industry flourished too, providing the material requirements of war: guns, cannons, and ammunition. As an iron molder, George was kept very busy.

By the time the North won the war and peace was declared in 1865, George and Mary had four young children. Memphis entered a period of prosperity: As the railroad grew to stretch across the continent, foundries were in ever greater demand, and the frenzied rate of factory production the war had spurred barely slowed. More people than ever before worked in factories and the idea of workers organizing to form unions was gaining popularity. George began working as a full-time paid organizer for the Iron Molders Union. His job, promoting the union and persuading people to join, took him on numerous travels throughout Tennessee and neighboring states. Though he was often gone for weeks at a time, leaving her alone to care for their babies, Mary encouraged his work. She supported the union and looked forward to the stories George would tell about the workers on his return to Memphis.

Then, in 1867, tragedy struck Memphis. After an unusually rainy spring left stagnant puddles of water and swampy creeks everywhere, the town endured the

*With its location on the Mississippi River and its network of railroads, Memphis, Tennessee, was an ideal center for transporting military supplies during the Civil War. For an iron molder like George Jones, this meant steady employment.*

hottest summer in memory. Under these conditions, mosquitoes bred rapidly, and by midsummer swarms of them had infested Memphis. People did not realize it at the time, but the mosquitoes carried the virus that causes the deadly disease called yellow fever. A cure for the easily spread disease had yet to be discovered, and before long the town was experiencing a full-fledged epidemic.

A painful and horrible disease, yellow fever started with fever and chills. Its unfortunate victims turned yellow, vomited black bile, and eventually were unable to eat. A few days later, they died. When word of this illness spread through Memphis, wealthy residents fled the city for the mountains, clogging the city streets with their carriages in a panic to get out. The less well-to-do, including the Jones family, had no alternative but to stay and risk their lives.

All churches and schools were closed; houses where the illness struck were quarantined and declared off-limits. Believing that smoke could ward off the disease, city officials had sulfur torches placed on the street corners. Choking clouds of black smoke engulfed the city and the rotten stench of sulfur and burning tar permeated the air. Horse-drawn wagons rolled through the streets at night, stopping at houses to collect the dead.

One by one, over several weeks, each of Mary and George's children caught the fever and died. Shortly after, George became ill and died too. Somehow, Mary sur-

### "Convictions and a Voice"

*Mother Jones was fiercely independent, strong, and determined. These qualities sustained her. In his book* Mother Jones Speaks, *labor historian Philip Foner describes Jones's indomitable spirit.*

"Throughout her career, Mother Jones had to face the cry that she represented anarchy, insurrection, socialism, and violence while the operators and employers in general represented law and order. She was called 'the most dangerous woman in America.'. . . But the opinion of employers and their agents did not matter to her. She ignored the attacks and went where danger was greatest—crossing militia lines, spending weeks in damp prisons, incurring the wrath of governors, presidents, and coal operators, as she devoted her life to the American labor movement, helping organize workers all over the United States and even in Canada—child textile workers, streetcar men, steel workers, metal miners, women in breweries, and women in the garment trades, but above all her beloved coal miners. She did this with the only tools she needed: 'convictions and a voice.'"

vived. "All about my house I could hear weeping and the cries of delirium," Mary remembered later. "I sat alone through nights of grief. No one came to me. No one could. Other homes were as stricken as mine. All day long, all night long, I heard the grating of the wheels of the death cart."[7] The local chapter of the Iron Molders Union held a meeting in George's honor, and paid funeral expenses for him and the children.

Though she could no longer do anything to help her own family, Mary applied for a permit to nurse others. She went into the quarantined homes and bathed and fed the sick. She cared for children whose parents were sick and she sat with the dying, providing what comfort she could. Then in December, with the first heavy frost, the mosquitoes died and, mercifully, the plague ended, having killed more than two hundred people.

There was no reason for Mary to remain in Memphis. Staying in the city that held such painful memories and where she had lost so much must have been unthinkable. So, with a modest sum of money George's union local had raised for her, she decided to move to Chicago, a bustling city that seemed to promise great opportunity. She planned to start a dressmaking business and a new life there.

## Great Chicago Fire

Chicago in 1868 was the busiest, fastest growing city in the nation. Like Memphis, it had been a trading and shipping center during the Civil War. Fortunes had been made there in meat packing, manufacturing, the railroad, and other industries. Af-

ter the war, the city continued to be a hub of industry and activity. More than two hundred trains came into or left Chicago each day, carrying goods to the rest of the nation. The owners of the railroads and the factories profited greatly from all this production: These new millionaire industrialists built lavish mansions and lived in great luxury on Chicago's North Shore along Lake Michigan. On the city's west side, amid slaughterhouses and belching factories, overcrowded tenements and rickety one-room shanties housed the masses of factory workers and the poor.

Mary found a storefront with a back room she could live in, and went to work as a seamstress. Before long she was busy again, her customers, the wealthy residents of Chicago's North Shore. Mary often went to work in their opulent homes, where she sewed ball gowns and party dresses for the women. Sitting in their living rooms, she could not help but notice the dramatic contrast between their lives and the lives of the poor. She recorded her observations in her autobiography:

> Often while sewing for the lords and barons who lived in magnificent houses along the Lake Shore Drive, I would look out the plate glass windows and see the poor, shivering wretches, jobless and hungry, walking along the frozen lake front. The contrast of their condition with that of the tropical comfort of the people for whom I sewed was painful to me. My employers seemed neither to notice nor to care.[8]

Though she often wished there was something she could do to help the poor, Mary's energy in the next few years was consumed by the demands of starting a new business and supporting herself.

*Fire rages through Chicago in 1871. The devastating fire left thousands, including Jones, without a home.*

Then, on the night of October 8, 1871, tragedy once more changed the course of Mary's life. It had not rained in Chicago in months and the city, with its many wooden streets and sidewalks, was as dry as a tinderbox. In a back-alley barn in the west-end Chicago slums, a cow tipped over a lantern and set fire to the hay. The barn burst into flames and, helped along by a hot dry wind, the flames shot through the streets, igniting fences, sidewalks, houses, and factories made entirely of wood. A watchman spotted the fire but, misjudging its location, gave the wrong signal, so fire-fighters were slow to respond. Soon an inferno raged, unchecked, through the west end of Chicago. Driven by strong winds, the fire spread to the city's North Shore, engulfing the homes of rich and poor alike.

When it was finally put out three days later, the Great Chicago Fire had claimed nearly three hundred lives, destroyed thousands of buildings, caused nearly $200 million in damages, and left ninety thousand people homeless. One of them was Mary Jones. She had joined the thousands of others who evacuated their homes and sought safety from the fire on the shores of Lake Michigan. There they camped without food for a day and a half, until donations from around the country began to pour in. When the flames were finally extinguished and the thick smoke cleared, people learned the terrible extent of the damage.

Mary's shop had been reduced to a pile of charred and blackened debris. Without her bolts of fabric and her sewing equipment, Mary no longer had a business. The back room of the shop was gone too, so she no longer had a home. For the second time in just a few years, she faced the loss of everything she had. Now in her early forties, she would have to start again from nothing and make a new life for herself. And this time she did not have the financial or emotional support of George's union to help get her on her feet. The clothes on her back were all that she had. What could the future possibly hold for Mary Jones?

# Chapter

## 2 An Instinct to Break the Chains

I belong to a class who have been robbed, exploited, and plundered down through many long centuries, and because I belong to that class I have an instinct to go and help break the chains.

—Mother Jones,
*The Autobiography of Mother Jones*

Jones's first step, as before in the face of tragedy, was to volunteer to help others. Donations of food and clothing for the Chicago fire victims were arriving daily from all over the United States and the goods had to be distributed somehow. The task of rebuilding what the fire had destroyed was enormous. Jones joined other volunteers and organized a soup kitchen. She helped to find lodging for the many homeless. A local church, St. Mary's, opened its doors as a shelter, and she moved in there temporarily.

Through her volunteer work, Mary came into contact with hundreds of working people. Occasionally, she met an iron molder who had worked with her late husband, George, or knew of him from his days with the Iron Molders Union. These encounters bolstered her spirits and gave her a sense of solidarity. She was beginning to forge connections that would give

her strength and encouragement, something she needed to rebuild her life.

Sometimes, after a long day spent volunteering, Jones went for a leisurely walk through the burned-out blocks in the neighborhood surrounding the church. This was her time for greeting friends and

*A young victim of the Great Chicago Fire weeps as she stands amidst the embers of her destroyed home. Jones's first reaction to the disaster was to help others.*

acquaintances. Passing by a run-down, fire-scorched building one evening, she spotted someone she knew and stopped to chat. He was guarding the doorway to a dilapidated building where a secret meeting was in progress. After they talked briefly, he invited Jones inside to listen to the meeting. She slipped in the door and found a seat in the back.

## The Knights of Labor

Jones had stumbled on a meeting of a newly formed union, the Noble Order of the Knights of Labor. The members were meeting in secret that night because at the time workers who belonged to unions could be fired or, worse, "blacklisted"— their names put on a list circulated among employers to ensure that no union members got hired anywhere again. Many employers wanted to keep workers from coming together to share their complaints and talk about solutions because they knew this was the workers' first step toward gaining some control over their often miserable working conditions. A factory boss could easily fire a solitary worker who spoke up. Hundreds of workers objecting together would be harder to ignore. Employers knew they would lose power and possibly some of their large profits if the union took hold.

The Knights had originated in Philadelphia in 1869 and spread rapidly to other cities. They were the most idealistic unionists of their day. Unlike other fledgling unions that focused exclusively on one trade, admitting only bricklayers, for example, the Knights wanted to include all workers: skilled and unskilled, black and white, male and female. They believed that workers stood to gain the most if all of them were united, regardless of gender, ethnicity, or occupation.

The Knights held radical views. They opposed the wage-system approach to the economy, whereby some people owned factories or mines and paid other people wages to work in them. The Knights believed that this system gave factory owners, who set wages themselves and were free to replace workers for any reason or at any time, too much power. Instead they favored a cooperative system, where workers owned and ran businesses together and shared equally in the profits. The Knights also opposed striking as a means of resistance. Because they often forced businesses to shut down altogether, strikes could be remarkably effective in forcing owners to agree to employees' demands. But the Knights disapproved of the violence that often accompanied strikes and thought workers could accomplish more by persuading the government to legislate reform. They emphasized education and peaceful solution, even if that meant that any change would be gradual.

Jones was inspired by the exciting and revolutionary ideas she heard at the Knights meeting that night. They grabbed her attention and aroused her deepest indignation. They stirred her memories, from her earliest days as the daughter of an Irish peasant turned railroad worker, to her marriage to a hardworking union organizer, to her own observations of injustice. She thought about the disparities between the lives of the rich and the poor she witnessed while working as a seamstress for Chicago's wealthy elite. Her own past and present struggles as a worker, and the struggles of working people every-

*Terrence Powderly, who would become the president of the Knights of Labor for more than ten years, was impressed with Jones's engaging speaking style and her knowledge of labor history. The two started a friendship that lasted all their lives.*

where, brought into sharper focus, she decided that night to become a member of the Knights.

## Apprenticeship

Although ultimately they would be the first union to do so, the Knights were not yet admitting women when Jones first approached them for membership. But she was told that she was welcome to volunteer her support and to attend meetings. Soon, she was doing both regularly. She accompanied the Knights on weekend outings, when they held picnics in the woods. She began venturing to the different sections of Chicago, talking to workers about the Knights, explaining who they were and what they were trying to do. To support herself, she worked as a seamstress again, using a sewing machine donated by the city after the fire as part of the relief ef-

fort. But all of her energy was focused on her volunteer work as an unofficial organizer for the Knights of Labor.

Something important for Jones was revealed at the Knights of Labor meetings she attended. They were lively affairs where people engaged in vigorous and heated debate, sometimes for hours. She found herself joining right in on the arguments, and in so doing discovered that she had a special ability for public speaking. Her presence was undeniably magnetic. She seemed a born persuader. During one meeting, she so impressed the designated speaker with her comments and her grasp of labor history that he made a point of introducing himself to her afterward. He was Terrence Powderly, who would become president of the Knights for more than a decade. Powderly and Jones became close friends. Although they disagreed completely on many issues related to labor—Powderly detested strikes, for example, whereas Jones placed great faith in them—the friendship lasted, supporting and sustaining them both for the rest of their lives.

Participating in these meetings of the Knights, Jones sharpened her speaking skills and learned much about labor organizations. The 1870s and 1880s were a period of apprenticeship for her. Her involvement with the Knights provided the training ground for what would become her life's work. Years later she wrote, "From the time of the Chicago Fire I became more and more engrossed in the labor struggle and I decided to take an active part in the efforts of the working people to better the conditions under which they worked and lived."[9] Having made that decision, Jones immersed herself in the practice of her new profession.

Her whereabouts during the 1870s and into the next decade are uncertain; just emerging on the labor scene, Jones was not yet a public figure. She may have traveled to San Francisco, where a growing socialist movement may have influenced her political views. Some newspaper accounts from the period suggest she traveled to Europe in 1873 and again in 1881 to study the conditions of workers in England, Germany, and France. She apparently used Chicago as a home base for a time, particularly while she established herself with the Knights, but after the Great Fire she never truly had a permanent home again. Thereafter, her home, she often said, was "wherever there is a fight."

From the Great Fire on, Mary Jones was busy learning all she could about the issues that would absorb her and drive her for the rest of her life. A number of early labor confrontations made a deep impression on her, emphasizing the plight of workers and the potential of unions to effect change and improve working conditions. She may have played minor roles in some of these confrontations, but for the most part she was a witness, gathering information, gleaning knowledge, and making and shaping her own observations. In the troubling days of the 1870s and 1880s, there was plenty to observe.

## The Panic of 1873

Two years after the Great Chicago Fire, a catastrophe of a different sort occurred, this time affecting the entire nation. In what came to be called the Panic of 1873, a leading brokerage house, Jay Cooke & Co., went bankrupt and shut down, causing a chain reaction of failures among hundreds of smaller banks. There was widespread financial collapse and the country was plunged into an economic depression practically overnight. Businesses that depended on the banks had no choice but to close, five thousand of them by the year's end. Factories closed and workers lost their jobs. By the following spring, four million people were out of work.

Hunger and unemployment took their heavy toll. Many lost their homes and were forced to live on the streets. People died of starvation in San Francisco, Chicago, New York, and other cities. Across America, people demanded food and jobs in mass protest demonstrations. When these protests threatened to erupt into violence, police and state militias quickly and sometimes violently suppressed them. As the decade rolled on, unemployment and poverty rose while wages fell.

*Stockholders scramble to sell their shares before the stock exchange shuts its doors. The Panic of 1873 quickly drove the country into economic despair.*

One of the industries hardest hit by the depression was the railroad. With the Panic of 1873, construction of new lines was halted and existing lines were forced to lower their operating costs. The wealthy industrialists who owned the railroads did not allow the depression to cut into their profits, however; they simply paid their employees less and required them to work harder. Over the next few years, the owners cut employee wages several times, fired thousands of workers, and required those still working to take on double their loads at the same pay. Employees put in fifteen-to-eighteen-hour days for $5 or $10 a week. Many were maimed or killed by collapsed trestles or corroded boilers because owners refused to spend money on necessary repairs. Through it all, the railroad owners seemed arrogant and indifferent to the suffering of the workers. Typical among them was industrialist Jay Gould, who, when asked if he was worried his workers might rebel against him, cruelly replied, "I can hire one half of the working class to kill the other half."[10]

*The Pennsylvania railroad workers' strike culminates in Pittsburgh with massive destruction, fire, and riots.*

## On Strike!

Jay Gould badly misunderstood and underestimated his workers, however. When a group of railroad owners met and decided to cut workers' wages by another 10 percent in 1877, the fourth time in a few years, the workers had finally had enough. On hearing the news, more than a thousand workers in Martinsburg, West Virginia, took control of the railroad depot and refused to let any trains enter or leave. The townspeople, angered by increased fares and sympathetic to the workers' predicament, joined in, as did the workers' wives and mothers. Confronted

by this angry crowd of thousands, the police were unable to regain control of the depot. The next day West Virginia's governor sent in the state militia, but many of the soldiers refused to fight and instead put down their guns in a gesture of sympathy and joined the crowd of protesters. Then the governor turned to President Rutherford Hayes, who sent four hundred federal soldiers to intervene.

Meanwhile, word of the rebellion in Martinsburg spread and within three days railroad workers in train yards all across the country walked off their jobs, refusing to go back to work unless the new pay cut was cancelled. The strike reached a climax in Pittsburgh, a railroad hub, where workers gathered on the tracks, just as they had done in Martinsburg, and refused to let through any but mail and passenger trains.

At this point, Mary Jones arrived in Pittsburgh, eager to help the strikers. Striking workers often stand or march together in picket lines, forming a human barrier to prevent strikebreakers, people newly hired to do the striking workers' jobs, from getting into the factory. Jones joined the picket lines. She and other volunteers helped collect and distribute food for the workers' families. As in Martinsburg, the local militia refused to use their guns against the Pittsburgh strikers, joining them instead. So the governor of Pennsylvania ordered state troops sent from Philadelphia. As the troops approached the huge crowd, preparing to disperse them, some boys threw stones,

and the soldiers opened fire, killing twenty-six of the demonstrators, among them some children.

The crowd of strikers, now more than 20,000 strong, became enraged. In retaliation, they forced the soldiers into a Pennsylvania Railroad roadhouse, then set train cars ablaze and sent them racing down the track toward the roadhouse. Amid bellowing smoke and bright orange flames, the soldiers burst out of the roadhouse and fled into the nearby streets. Rioting continued through the night: By morning, 79 buildings and 105 locomotives were destroyed, causing the railroad $5 to $10 million in damages.

The strike finally ended when President Hayes, professing concern for the nation's security, sent in federal troops to keep peace. The railroad workers were ordered to return to their jobs, but only a

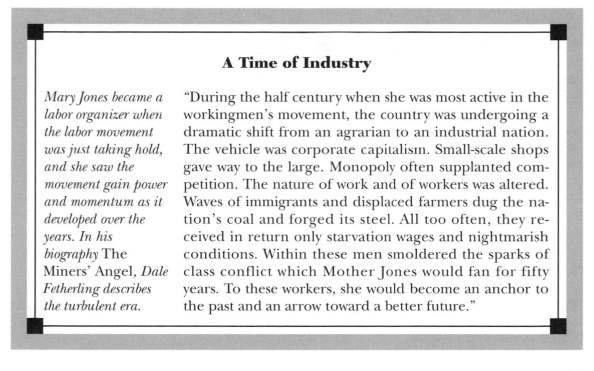

### A Time of Industry

*Mary Jones became a labor organizer when the labor movement was just taking hold, and she saw the movement gain power and momentum as it developed over the years. In his biography* The Miners' Angel, *Dale Fetherling describes the turbulent era.*

"During the half century when she was most active in the workingmen's movement, the country was undergoing a dramatic shift from an agrarian to an industrial nation. The vehicle was corporate capitalism. Small-scale shops gave way to the large. Monopoly often supplanted competition. The nature of work and of workers was altered. Waves of immigrants and displaced farmers dug the nation's coal and forged its steel. All too often, they received in return only starvation wages and nightmarish conditions. Within these men smoldered the sparks of class conflict which Mother Jones would fan for fifty years. To these workers, she would become an anchor to the past and an arrow toward a better future."

*The Pennsylvania strike of 1877 quickly turned into a national strike. Railroad workers in Baltimore, Maryland, are gunned down by soldiers as they strike against unfair working practices.*

handful saw any change in their working environment. For most of them, the wage cut that had prompted the whole violent episode remained in effect, as did the long hours and the dangerous working conditions.

Nonetheless, the strike had a powerful effect. So strong was the workers' desire for change that what began as a local dispute had quickly and spontaneously turned into the first national strike in U.S. history. Workers discovered what they might accomplish if they pooled their efforts—if they came together as a union, in other words—a realization that was vital to the growth of the labor movement. With that insight, thousands would join unions in the days ahead. The fact that the U.S. government had intervened not for the workers, but on behalf of the railroad companies, further underscored the need for workers to organize. If working men and women could not trust or depend upon the government to protect their interests, they believed, they had only each other and the unions they could organize to rely on.

Employers responded to this show of workers' potential strength by resolving to maintain a firm grip over their employees. They pushed for laws banning unions and tried to increase their influence over state militias. They began to recruit their own private guards and detectives. "That tumultuous year, 1877, marked a turning point in the struggle between capital and labor in the United States," writes historian Irving Werstein. "Much of the violence that scarred the American labor scene for decades after had its origins in these dramatic events of the 70's."[11] The Great Upheaval, as the railroad strike of 1877 came to be called, was a watershed event. It helped to set the machinery of change in motion, and from then on, there would be no stopping it.

The Pennsylvania Railroad strike was of personal significance to Mary Jones. As one of her earliest labor experiences, it made a deep impression on her. Her presence in Pittsburgh as an observer and participant intensified the already strong feelings she had in favor of the labor movement. She saw firsthand what solidarity could do for the downtrodden at the same time that she comprehended the magnitude of the resistance working people faced. She did not believe that the fire had been set by strikers, though a number of them were being charged with arson in a controversial and very public trial. The experience taught her a bitter lesson. "I knew the strikers personally. . . . I knew they disciplined those who committed acts of violence," she recalled years later. "Then and there I learned in the early part of my career that labor must bear the cross for others' sins, must be the vicarious sufferer for the wrong others do."[12]

# Haymarket Square

Another early and important labor confrontation, the Haymarket Square riot of 1886, had a similarly profound effect on Jones, though in this incident, too, the part she played was relatively minor. In the mid-1880s, the "eight-hour-day movement" was gaining popularity and working-class support around the country. At the time, many industries required men and women to work fourteen and even sixteen hours a day. Those workers advocating the eight-hour day were willing to work for less pay in exchange for a shorter day spent at the factory.

In Chicago, members of the Anarchist Party became involved in the movement, alienating disapproving politicians, businessmen, and law enforcement. Anarchists believe that government exists only to protect the interests of the rich and powerful, and is indifferent or hostile to working people. Their goal, then as now, was to abolish government and return control to the people. Because they sometimes resorted to violence to spread their message, anarchists of the day caused a great deal of controversy and fear among the public.

On May 1, 1886, nearly sixty thousand people, many anarchists included, demonstrated in Chicago in support of the eight-hour day. Despite tensions over the anarchist involvement, the event was peaceful. Two days later, however, in an unrelated strike at Chicago's McCormick Harvester plant, police opened fire and killed four strikers on a picket line. The killings outraged the anarchists and Chicago's labor union leaders and they called for a protest meeting the following evening in Haymarket Square, a public

*Dynamite suddenly explodes among the police at an 1886 protest meeting at Haymarket Square. The riot that followed resulted in eleven deaths and hundreds of injuries.*

gathering place. The meeting was widely publicized and nearly three thousand people attended to listen to the anarchists and other leaders speak out against police brutality. While dozens of police looked on, the meeting wore on peacefully. When it began to rain at 10 P.M., most of the crowd, including Mary Jones, went home. As the final speaker took the stand, police crowded in and ordered the remaining protesters to go home. Just then a dynamite bomb exploded in the police ranks. Immediately, police began firing on the assemblage. Many in the crowd were armed, and they fired back. In the hail of

gunfire that ensued, seven police and four workers were killed. Hundreds more were injured.

The event caused a huge public outcry. Alarmed Chicago city officials called a state of emergency and canceled all public meetings. The eight-hour-day movement was banned, its leaders around the country arrested. Labor unions, too, were blamed for the violence and came under attack by newspapers, civic and religious leaders, and the public. Although the identity of the bomb thrower was never learned and no proof linked the anarchists to the crime, eight well-known anarchists were tried and sentenced to death. Four of them were hanged, one committed suicide in prison, and three were sentenced to life in prison. "The workers' cry for justice was drowned in the shriek for revenge,"[13] Mary Jones wrote years later. The Knights of Labor, because it renounced strikes and violence, refused to come to the aid of the men charged with murder or to support the eight-hour-day movement, further angering Jones and the many workers who felt betrayed by the turn of events.

When a new governor of Illinois assumed office six years later, he conducted his own careful investigation into the Haymarket affair. Governor John P. Altgeld found that the eight convicted men had all been entirely innocent, and he freed the anarchists who still remained in jail. He disclosed evidence that they had been framed and that police had threatened and bribed witnesses and planted bombs to make it look as though the men were guilty. These revelations were angrily denied by Chicago's businessmen and law enforcement agencies and led directly to Governor Altgeld's political demise. But they endeared the governor to Mary Jones for life. Governor Altgeld "committed political suicide by his brave action," she

wrote, "but he is remembered by all those who love truth and those who have the courage to confess it."[14]

## Drastic Measures

The Haymarket affair, now an important event in American labor history, had a profound effect on Jones. The Knights' seeming indifference to the whole episode moved her to sever her ties to the organization and probably led directly to her taking a more active part in future labor conflicts. However much she agreed with the Knights' lofty goals of radical social reform, she had lost patience with their reluctance to engage in the grittier realities of strikes and guns and violence. The workers she had met and talked to were desperate and hungry and had families to provide for. They could not wait for a distant future day when things would be better for them; they needed an immediate change in their lives. If Jones had ever believed—as most Knights did—that peaceful means, education, and government assistance alone could bring about that change, she was no longer able to think so. More drastic measures were clearly in order.

# 3 The Coal Miners

I am not afraid of the pen, or the scaffold, or the sword. I will tell the truth wherever I please.

—Mother Jones,
*The Autobiography of Mother Jones*

Over her long career, Mary Jones organized workers from all trades and walks of life. She identified most strongly, however, with coal miners and primarily championed their cause. She reserved a special sympathy for miners, perhaps because many of them were, like herself, Irish immigrants, or descendants of other recent immigrants. In 1900 she joined the ranks of a powerful new union recently formed for coal miners, the United Mine Workers of America (UMWA). For the next thirty years, she traveled wherever the UMWA sent her in the fight for workers' rights. Her job was to persuade workers to join the union, which she did most commonly by holding incendiary meetings, explaining to the workers that although they were powerless as individuals, if they came together as a group—if they joined the union—they could succeed in making their demands heard.

As Jones learned, the life of a coal miner could indeed be miserable. Miners worked underground for twelve and four-

*The emblem of the United Mine Workers of America. Jones joined the union in 1900 and took an active part in recruiting other members.*

*The hazards of mining were tremendous, and mining accidents were frequent. (Left) A mine explosion leaves miners and their horse buried beneath rubble. (Below) Miners remove two injured workers from a collapsed cave.*

teen hours a day, six days a week, in back-breaking, dangerous conditions. To get to the richest coal veins, they had to crawl through dark tunnels to cramped caves, often no more than three feet high. Crouching, they picked and shoveled the black coal all day, loading it onto carts to be pulled out by donkeys or, if the tunnel was especially narrow, dogs. Frequently, the roofs of these caves collapsed without warning, crushing workers or suffocating them before help could arrive. Explosions were common too: Methane gas released when coal was dug needed only a spark to ignite a fierce explosion. Those lives that escaped accidents were often shortened instead by the fine coal dust that coated the men's lungs and made them ill.

## Company Towns

Because the mines were usually located in remote, mountainous places, far from ex-

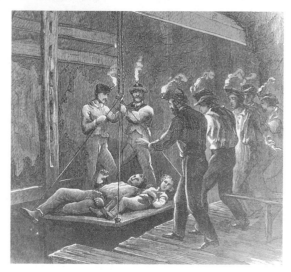

isting towns, coal companies often built their own towns near mining operations. These "company towns" varied from place to place, but usually included houses, a school and a store, a church, and sometimes a medical clinic. Because the company literally owned the town, it wielded enormous influence over what went on there. The town doctor, schoolteacher,

*A 1910 photo of a mining town in Scranton, Pennsylvania. The mining companies that built and owned the towns where their workers lived exerted control over residents by regulating where the residents could buy food and other necessities.*

and preacher were all hired and controlled by the company. The company set the prices in its stores—called "pluck me" stores by the miners because the prices there were so high—and then denied miners the option of shopping for lower prices elsewhere by paying them in scrip instead of cash. Paper certificates printed by the company, scrip was worthless everywhere except at a company store.

Because miners' wages were so low, many families ran out of money before payday. Encouraged by the company to buy on credit, these families were constantly in debt, unable to save the money they would need to move away in search of a better job. So they remained where they were, and the sons followed their fathers into the mines in a bleak cycle of poverty and despair.

## Miners Dub Her "Mother"

Not long after joining the UMWA, Jones began making a name for herself. In the coal-mining regions of the country—Pennsylvania, the Colorado Rockies, rural West Virginia—word was spreading of a white-haired, sweet-faced old woman whose "earnestness would carry conviction to a steel magnet itself."[15] She began to show up in newspaper accounts described as a "conspicuous and colorful organizer, particularly of the wives."[16] Mining communities eagerly anticipated her arrival. She would appear in their somber small towns, a delicate-looking figure in her Victorian black dress and bonnet, and in a flurry of activity rouse the miners and their families from their tired resignation. She would organize a meeting to be held at an old abandoned barn or in a field outside town after dark. Finding a secret, out-of-the-way location for the meeting was important, because the miners could be fired if the company boss found out they were even considering joining a union.

The purpose of these meetings was to educate the workers about the union and what it could do for them, but although they were informational, the meetings were far from boring or businesslike affairs. Most often, they were charged with emotion and excitement. When the deceptively fragile-looking Jones took the floor, she underwent a complete transformation, from a mild-mannered and unimposing grandmotherly figure to a passionate Joan of Arc. Her speech became, in the words of one reporter, "pyrotechnic, enthusiastic, spectacular."[17] In a strong,

---

## A Typical Speech

*Mother Jones was a powerful and persuasive speaker, skilled at drawing out people's emotions and sparking their desire to change their lives. In the following account, reprinted in Linda Atkinson's* Mother Jones, *a reporter for the* Boston Herald *describes hearing Mother Jones speak to a group of miners in West Virginia in the spring of 1901.*

" 'Has anyone ever told you, my children,' she said, 'about the lives you are living here, so that you may understand how it is you pass your days on earth? Have you told each other about it and thought it over among yourselves, so that you might imagine a brighter day and begin to bring it to pass? If no one has done so, I will do it for you today. Let us consider this together, for I am one of you, and I know what it is to suffer.'

So the old lady, standing very quietly, in her deep, far-reaching voice, painted a picture of a life of a miner from his boyhood to his old age. It was a vivid picture. She talked of the first introduction a boy had to those dismal caves under the earth, dripping with moisture, often so low that he must crawl into the coal veins, must lie on his back to work. She told how miners stood bent over until the back ached too much to straighten, or in sulphur water that ate through the shoes and made sores on the flesh; how their hands became cracked and their nails broken off in the quick; how the bit of bacon and beans in the dinner pail failed to stop the craving of their empty stomachs, and the thought of the barefoot children at home and the sick mother was all too dreary to make the home-going a cheerful one. . . . 'You pity yourselves,' she said, 'but you do not pity your brothers, or you would stand together to help one another.' And then, in an impassioned vein she called upon them to awaken their minds so that they might live another life. As she ceased speaking, men and women looked at each other with shamed faces, for almost everyone had been weeping."

low voice that carried easily to the farthest row of seats, she rebuked her audience for their apathy and their apparent acceptance of their hard lot. "If you would just use your brains instead of your mouths, but you do not,"[18] she railed at one group of miners. Other times she called the men cowards who were afraid to fight back against their bosses. She could work the men into a frenzy or move them to tears.

But she never lacked compassion. Her speeches were meant to encourage the miners to face their employers with pride and to inspire them with visions of a better life. And, of course, to get them to join the union. Again and again she returned to that same message: Join the union and fight for a better way of life. No one seemed to understand the miners' troubles or inspire them quite like she did. They admired and adored her in return and affectionately dubbed her "Mother," a nickname that was to stick for the rest of her life, and the name by which she is known today.

Her activities were not limited to meetings, though, and Mother Jones's job was not of the eight-hours-at-the-office variety. To try to point to Mother Jones's job and then to her life, as though they were somehow separate, would be difficult. She immersed herself in her work, and it became her life. When she went to remote mountainous coal regions, she stayed with the miners' families, sharing their food and sleeping wherever there was a spare bed. She climbed down into the dark, damp mines where the men worked and sat with them in the taverns they frequented on their way home from work. She knew firsthand their wretched working and living conditions. Everywhere she went, she spoke out forcefully against the companies and their abhorrent practices. Her official job title was union organizer, but Mother Jones preferred to call what she did "hell-raising." She did it extremely well.

## The Mop and Broom Brigade

Stressful living and working conditions predominated throughout the coal-mining regions of the United States since the industry boom following the Civil War. In the early 1900s miners in Pennsylvania's coalfields were driven to do something about them. In addition to the usual grievances surrounding company towns, dangerous conditions, and low pay, Pennsylvania miners' low pay had been falling even lower. As miners' wages were based on the weight of the coal they mined, the workers suspected that the coal company was cheating them by underreporting the coal's true weight, but they had no way to verify this suspicion: The company had complete control over the weighing process and did not allow a miners' representative to monitor it.

Miners across the region decided to go on strike to protest weighing practices and other working conditions. Their morale was low, however, and the coal company had so far refused to make any concessions. It simply transported strikebreakers, insultingly called scabs by strikers, from distant towns and states to take the strikers' jobs. In the little town of Arnot, Pennsylvania, the miners were ready to give up. Dejected, they held a vote, and decided 130 to 19 to call off the strike and go back to work.

The very next day, Mother Jones arrived in town. She quickly organized one

## A Good Soul and a Lively Sense of Humor

*In this description from* The Miners' Angel, *John Brophy recalls meeting Mother Jones during the Arnot, Pennsylvania, coal strike. When they met, Brophy was a fifteen-year-old coal miner, but later he became an important labor leader in his own right.*

"She came into the mine one day and talked to us in the vernacular of the mines. How she got in I don't know; probably just walked in and defied anyone to stop her. . . . She would take a drink with the boys and spoke their idiom, including some pretty rough language when it came to talking about the bosses. This might have been considered a little fast in ordinary women, but the miners knew and respected her. They might think her a little queer, perhaps—it *was* odd kind of work for a woman in those days—but they knew she was a good soul. . . . She had a lively sense of humor—she could tell wonderful stories, usually at the expense of some boss, for she couldn't resist the temptation to agitate, even in a joke."

of the meetings she was becoming famous for, weaving into her speech all her most persuasive strategies, and turned the vote around. Then she came up with a plan. Seeing that the men were tired and demoralized, she decided to enlist the help of the strikers' wives and mothers. Gathering the women together, Jones told them to meet her early the next morning armed with mops, brooms, and pots and pans. Leave the babies at home with the men, she added.

Early the following morning, the "mop and broom brigade" set off for the mines, determined to chase the strikebreakers away. Mother Jones, looking for a woman to lead the procession, settled on an Irishwoman who, she wrote later, "had a most picturesque appearance. She had tied a little red fringed shawl over her wild red hair. Her face was red and her eyes were mad. I looked at her and felt that she could raise a rumpus."[19] The women gathered at the entrance to the mine and waited.

## A Successful Plan

When the strikebreakers appeared on the road, riding in wagons pulled by mules, the women began shouting and hollering and waving their brooms about. They rushed toward the men, banging their tin pans. Terrified by the noise and commotion, the mules bucked and kicked and started off down the road, followed closely by the alarmed strikebreakers. Their spirits bolstered by this success, and encouraged by a gleeful Mother Jones, the women began going daily to the mine entrance to repeat their performance and ensure that strikebreakers kept out of the mines. Organizing the miners' wives into a brigade proved to be so successful and popular a tactic that it eventually became something of a trademark for Mother Jones, and she relied on its effectiveness many times in coming years.

Jones took steps to further strengthen the strikers' resolve. For the next five months she traveled the northern Pennsylvania coalfields, from one camp to the next, urging the strikers to support each other and to hold out for victory. She organized marches throughout the region. Her days were long and arduous. She remembered later:

> Sometimes it was 12 or 1 o'clock in the morning when I would get home. Sometimes it was several degrees below zero. The winds whistled down the mountains and drove the sleet and snow in our faces. My hands and feet were often numb. We were all living on dry bread and black coffee. I slept in a room that never had a fire in it, and I often woke up in the morning to find snow covering the outside covers of the bed.[20]

Mother Jones's hard work paid off. After nine months, the company finally conceded to the workers' demands, and the strike was called off. That night, the miners and their families threw a jubilant victory and farewell party for Mother Jones at the opera house in Blossburg, Pennsylvania. Hundreds of miners walked from Arnot, five miles away, through the cold February snow to attend the celebration. Their wives and families came, even the babies, bundled tightly against the cold. The mood was joyous and the dancing and singing lasted well into the night. A UMWA official proclaimed that Mother

Jones had "snatched victory out of the very jaws of defeat."[21] Jones, deeply honored by the evening's tribute, left the area the next day encouraged and inspired. The Pennsylvania victory was a significant one, the union's most successful strike to date. And Mother Jones had played an indispensable part.

## The Kanawha Valley

Shortly after the success in Pennsylvania, the UMWA organized a new drive in West Virginia, where opposition to the union was the most extreme in the country. John Mitchell, president of the UMWA, asked Mother Jones to lead the strike effort in the southern coalfield of West Virginia. She was growing increasingly confident and successful, and under her leadership, the union began infiltrating the targeted southern section in the winter of 1902. In the Kanawha Valley, a key area, Mother Jones was responsible for starting two union locals. By spring, she sent a notice to union headquarters that read "I am having glorious meetings. The boys are responding to the high call, and I think we will give you the Kanawha River organized by the first of May."[22]

In the northern part of West Virginia, however, opposition to the union was unyielding and the news from there was grim. Those workers who did belong to the union were attacked and beaten at the hands of company guards. Frightened by the violence, most miners were reluctant to get involved with the union, and progress was slow. With Jones's courage and persuasive abilities in mind, John Mitchell appealed to her to go to the

When John Mitchell, president of the UMWA, needed a courageous person to undertake the dangerous mission of leading strike efforts in northern West Virginia, he called on Mother Jones.

guards and stepped up the violence. Shootings and beatings became daily occurrences. Attempts were made on the lives of union organizers.

Frightened miners stayed away from the union. But the companies increased their intimidation, approaching local judges seeking injunctions, legal orders forbidding people from holding meetings or making public speeches. Anyone caught violating an injunction could be arrested and jailed. The injunctions were designed specifically to prevent organizers like Mother Jones from having any contact whatsoever with the miners. But Jones simply ignored the injunctions; if she could not hold meetings or speak publicly, she could not do her job. She would just have to take her chances.

## "Goodbye, Boys; I'm Under Arrest"

northern region. "The coal operators there have evidently scared our boys," he wrote to her, "and of course with good reason, as they have brutally beaten some of them. I dislike to ask you always to take the dangerous fields, but I know that you are willing."[23]

Mother Jones was only too willing. She quickly packed her bags and left for northern West Virginia. Just after she arrived, the union organizer she was sent to assist was arrested, and Jones abruptly found herself in charge of the whole field. Then, in early June, a statewide strike began. More than half the miners in West Virginia walked off their jobs and moved out of their company-owned houses into temporary tent cities. In response the coal companies immediately hired more

A few weeks later, Mother Jones was addressing a workers' rally when she spotted marshals moving through the crowd. As they approached the platform, she told her audience "Goodbye, boys; I'm under arrest. I may have to go to jail." The marshals allowed her a few more words before they led her away. "Keep up this fight," she continued. "Don't surrender. Pay no attention to the injunction machine at Parkersburg. The federal judge is a scab anyhow. While you starve, he plays golf. While you serve humanity, he serves injunctions for the money powers."[24] Then Jones and eleven other organizers were put on a train for Parkersburg, where they were booked into the Wood County Jail. UMWA president John Mitchell sent word

## Mining Is Wretched Work

*Mother Jones immersed herself in the miners' lives and knew firsthand their oppressive living and working conditions. In this excerpt from her autobiography, she writes movingly about the coal miner's hardscrabble existence.*

"Mining at its best is wretched work, and the life and the surroundings of the miner are hard and ugly. His work is down in the black depths of the earth. He works alone in a drift. There can be little friendly companionship as there is in the factory; as there is among men who built bridges and houses, working together in groups. His work is dirty. Coal dust grinds itself into the skin, never to be removed. He becomes bent like a gnome.

His work is utterly fatiguing. Muscles and bones ache. His lungs breathe coal dust and the strange, damp air of places that are never filled with sunlight. His house is a poor makeshift, and there is little to encourage him to make it attractive. The company owns the ground it stands on, and the miner feels the precariousness of his hold. Around his house is mud and slush. Great mounds of culm, black and sullen, surround him. His children are perpetually grimy from play on the culm mounds. His wife struggles with dirt, with inadequate water supply, with small wages, with overcrowded shacks."

*Sitting alone in a dark underground mine, a thirteen-year-old worker waits for the next load of coal to come through.*

that the union protested the arrests and would seek a presidential pardon if necessary to free Mother Jones.

At the subsequent courtroom trial, the judge called the union organizers "vampires that live and fatten on the honest labor of coal miners." He lectured Mother Jones, telling her she had "strayed from the lines and paths which the Allwise Being intended her sex to pursue" and that if she wished to help "mankind in distress"[25] she ought to stick to charity work. In response she called the judge a scab, causing an uproar in the courtroom. She had done her duty, Mother Jones told him, and would do it again. Then, in a conciliatory tone, she added that she and the judge were both old and that she hoped they could become good friends and meet in heaven one day. At that, the courtroom audience burst into applause.

The other organizers were each sentenced to sixty days in jail, but the judge let Mother Jones go with a suspended sentence. If she was arrested again, he warned, the penalty would be severe. After the trial she returned to southern West Virginia, to the Kanawha Valley, where she found resistance to the strike and the union had intensified. Strikers were forbidden from buying goods at the company store. Company-hired guards carried out their own campaign of terror, brutally beating and even killing strikers. The union organizers faced great dangers as well: They were forced to spend many nights hiding out from company guards, sleeping on riverbanks or deep in the woods. "We could hear bullets whizz past us," Mother Jones recalled, "as we sat huddled between boulders, our black clothes making us invisible in the blackness of night."[26]

## The Stanaford Mountain Massacre

In the nearby Stanaford Mountain district there was an especially vicious attack. A group of strikers told Mother Jones how they chased away a deputy sheriff who had come to arrest them for loitering. She warned the men that the sheriff would probably be back with extra help. Be prepared to surrender, she advised, whether or not you are guilty, and do not give him an opportunity to use his gun. The sheriff did return in the night, with eighty armed men. They attacked the sleeping camp, killing eight miners while they slept and wounding twenty others.

Hearing the awful news the next morning, Mother Jones went immediately to the camp. "I pushed open the door [of a miner's shack]," she recalled years later. "On a mattress, wet with blood, lay a miner. His brains had been blown out while he slept." In another shack, Jones wrote, "a baby boy and his mother sobbed over the father's corpse. When the little fellow saw me, he said, 'Mother Jones, bring back my papa to me. I want to kiss him.'"[27]

To the union's dismay, this new height in brutality against the strikers went unnoticed, or at least unpunished. After the massacre, the Stanaford miners and their families lost heart and the strike collapsed in that district, and soon in others. By the fall of 1902 the strike was over across the state of West Virginia. It had been a complete failure, except in one district—the Kanawha Valley, where Mother Jones had spent most of her time. The strikers in the valley made several gains, including a nine-hour day, the right to shop where

*Jones's organizing efforts brought her face-to-face with danger and violence. Undaunted, she kept up her passionate fight for workers' rights.*

they wished, and, most significantly, the right to be represented by the union.

The impressive outcome at Kanawha Valley, due largely to Mother Jones's organizing efforts, was significant. Everywhere else in West Virginia, however, working conditions remained the same. Workers' pay was much lower than that of miners in other states, the hours spent working were longer, and the cost of living was higher.

The company operators paid close attention to those tactics that worked best in keeping the miners unorganized and made sure to keep them in place. Ten years would pass before a major strike was even attempted again in West Virginia. When the time came, Mother Jones would be there, and once more she would play a vital role. In the meantime, though, she became involved with a struggle of a rather different nature, one that would draw the attention of an entire nation.

# 4 March of the Mill Children

I was given work in the factory, and there I saw the children, little children working, the most heart-rending spectacle in all life. Sometimes it seemed to me I could not look at those silent little figures; that I must go north, to the grim coal fields, or to the Rocky Mountain camps, where the labor fight is at least fought by grown men.

—Mother Jones,
*The Autobiography of Mother Jones*

One bright June morning in 1903, Mother Jones met with a large, boisterous group of factory workers, employees of the textile mills on the outskirts of Philadelphia. Thousands of workers from the mills were going on strike for better pay and working conditions, and Mother Jones had come, as she so often did, to lend a hand. Only this time, something was different. The group of three hundred or so strikers gathering eagerly around Mother Jones for a planned march that morning consisted largely of children, some as young as six and seven years old.

A Pennsylvania law prohibited children under the age of thirteen from work-

*A girl labors at a spinning machine in a large textile factory. After Jones saw children working long hours for little pay in the mills, she crusaded for laws against child labor.*

ing in the mills, but no one had ever tried to enforce it. Mill owners were only too happy to hire children, who worked the same number of hours as adults, but for much less pay. Even had the law been enforced, many poverty-stricken parents were willing to lie about their children's ages to send them into the mills to earn the few extra dollars each week. Many families would likely have starved without the additional income.

## "Little Grey Ghosts"

Of all the injustices Mother Jones witnessed in her long life, nothing tugged at her heart quite so much as child labor. During the last years of the nineteenth century, more than a million American children spent their young lives working. They toiled in the cotton mills of the South and in the textile mills and coal mines farther north, entering the factories at daybreak and working until the sun began to set. The work they did was demanding and dangerous. Exhausted from lack of sleep and exercise, weary children often dozed on the job. Sometimes their hands and arms were caught in dangerous factory machinery and many suffered mutilated fingers, crushed hands, and broken bones.

Mother Jones, who saw lots of child laborers come into union headquarter offices in Philadelphia, called the children "little grey ghosts." "They were stooped little things," she wrote of them, "round shouldered and skinny."[28] Their backs were bent from hunching over their tasks all day, and their faces were worn and tired. Factory children looked old well before their time.

Labor historians point out that children began working in factories as soon as the first factories opened their doors. Before the advent of mass production, goods had been produced by craftspeople in limited quantities. Typically, all the members of a family were involved in the production of goods, each assigned specialized tasks and all working together in their homes or small shops. With the Industrial Revolution, however, production increased tremendously and factories opened to handle the increased volumes. Those who produced the goods, including the children, followed the work into factories. In Great Britain, children made up nearly the entire workforce in the silk factories and cotton mills. Children there helped with the coal production that was vital to all the new industry, entering the coal mines when they were six and working six days a week for twelve to eighteen hours a day. Coal mining, factory production, and the expanding railroad were booming businesses in the United States, too. Industrialists on the lookout for a cheap, plentiful labor pool saw that children fit those requirements.

Mother Jones knew something was fundamentally wrong when children spent their days working. They should be in school, she believed, or outdoors playing in the fresh air, not underground all day in the coal mines or deep in the recesses of a dangerous factory. Outraged that these children of the poor were being robbed of their childhoods, Mother Jones was determined to do what she could to help fight child labor. In the spring of 1903, when she learned of a strike in the Kensington textile mills outside Philadelphia in which at least ten thousand children were participating, she hurried to Pennsylvania.

*A weary young spinner poses for a photo in 1908. Outraged by the injustices of child labor, Jones organized a march on city hall to draw attention to the serious problem.*

## March on City Hall

Shortly after her arrival, Mother Jones asked three hundred of the children and their parents to join her on a march to protest child labor. The group gathered in Philadelphia's Independence Square on a June morning and set out. Jones led the factory children on a march of less than a mile, through the winding streets of Philadelphia and up to the steps of city hall, before which a large crowd had gathered in the public square. Mother Jones stepped to the front of the crowd, accompanied by a few of the girls and boys. She lifted one of them, a lightweight, bedraggled boy, onto a platform for the crowd to see. The boy's hand was mutilated, his fingers torn from the knuckle when they were caught in a factory weaving machine. She lifted more children over the heads of the crowd and pointed to their spindly arms and legs and their sunken chests.

"Philadelphia's mansions," she cried, "were built on the broken bones, the quivering hearts and drooping heads of these children! Their little lives [go out to] make wealth for others!"[29] Across the lawn, uneasy city officials watched the demonstration from the open windows of city hall. Spotting them, Jones called out, "Some day the workers will take possession of your city hall, and when we do, no child will be sacrificed on the altar of profit!" The officials quickly closed their windows, Jones recalled, "just as they had closed their eyes and hearts."[30] Reporters mingled through the crowd, busily taking notes.

The next day the story hit the papers as far away as New York City. Reporters described the march and editorials condemned child labor, just as Mother Jones had hoped they would. And then, after a day or two, the clamor died down as abruptly as it had arisen. Jones confronted local newspaper reporters, demanding to know why they did not address the issue of child labor more often in their pages. They told her that the mill owners were part owners of the newspapers, too, and strongly discouraged reporters from writing about the children.

That was just the sort of response that outraged Mother Jones. Opposition always seemed to urge her on and inspire her to work twice as hard. Something more had to be done, she knew, to draw attention to the children and publicize their plight. She needed a plan that would cause a bigger uproar, ideally something that would force the government to act against child labor. As usual, it did not take Mother Jones long to come up with an idea.

## The Children's Crusade

Philadelphia's historic Liberty Bell had recently been taken on a tour of the country so Americans everywhere could see it. The undertaking had been a great success and thousands of people had turned out to view the Liberty Bell. Why not, thought Mother Jones, organize a tour of the mill children so that thousands of people could see the children and hear their stories first-hand? Such an experience would certainly arouse people's sympathies and educate them about the evils of child labor.

Mother Jones proposed the idea at the next textile union meeting. She and a group of children would walk the route the Liberty Bell took from Philadelphia to New York City, then detour to Oyster Bay on Long Island to the summer home of President Theodore Roosevelt. Walking no more than ten miles a day, they would plan to complete the 125-mile journey in a

*Before child labor laws were implemented, young workers faced sixteen-hour workdays and dangerous conditions. Here, a child stands bent from years of premature toil in the mines.*

few weeks' time. A horse-drawn wagon would be available for those children who wished to ride; another would carry the group's food and supplies. They would pack tents for camping out, but Jones would arrange for the children to sleep indoors whenever possible. At certain scheduled stops, they would stage a demonstration—the children might sing and play instruments, and Mother Jones would give one of her fiery speeches—and solicit donations for the textile strike. But the main purpose of the march would be to draw the attention of the country to the problem of child labor and to appeal directly to the president of the United States. Mother Jones wanted his support for federal legislation banning child labor.

Some parents were enthusiastic about the idea and a number of adults volunteered to come along and help out. On July 7 some three hundred children and adults started out on the march with Mother Jones. A group of children dressed as Revolutionary War soldiers took the lead. One child played the fife, another the drum. Other children carried signs and banners. "We want to go to school" read one. "More schools, less hospitals" and "We want time to play" read others.[31] Fortunately the weather was sunny and warm and the marchers' spirits were high. That night, the group stopped at Torresdale Park outside Philadelphia and enjoyed a picnic. The adults put out huge plates of bread and cheese. Local farmers donated fresh fruit and vegetables and milk. Later that evening, Mother Jones spoke to a crowd of nearly a thousand who came to the park to meet the marchers and wish them well.

Over the next few days, however, the weather turned swelteringly hot, and Mother Jones thought it best to send a number of children back to Kensington rather than have them walk in the heat. Some of the adults tired or quickly lost interest in the march, and they dropped out or went home too. Soon fewer than a hundred marchers remained, but they straggled on, caked with dust and breathing hard in the oppressively humid air. As the procession approached Morrisville, a town on the banks of the Delaware River, a handful of the boys broke away to jump

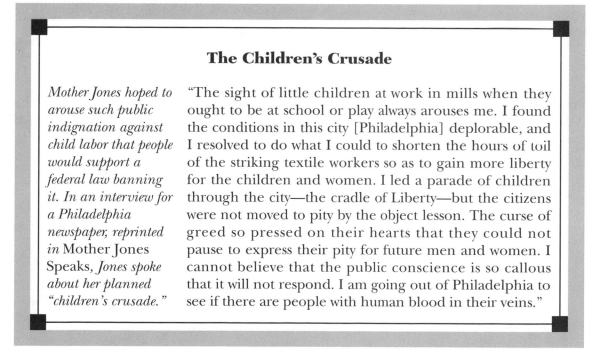

**The Children's Crusade**

*Mother Jones hoped to arouse such public indignation against child labor that people would support a federal law banning it. In an interview for a Philadelphia newspaper, reprinted in* Mother Jones Speaks, *Jones spoke about her planned "children's crusade."*

"The sight of little children at work in mills when they ought to be at school or play always arouses me. I found the conditions in this city [Philadelphia] deplorable, and I resolved to do what I could to shorten the hours of toil of the striking textile workers so as to gain more liberty for the children and women. I led a parade of children through the city—the cradle of Liberty—but the citizens were not moved to pity by the object lesson. The curse of greed so pressed on their hearts that they could not pause to express their pity for future men and women. I cannot believe that the public conscience is so callous that it will not respond. I am going out of Philadelphia to see if there are people with human blood in their veins."

into the cool refreshing water. In no time, the rest of the group joined them for a spontaneous bath and swim. Mother Jones sent word to union headquarters that "the children are very happy. They have plenty to eat, some for the first time in their lives. They enjoy the fresh air. I think that when the strike is over, and they must go back to the mills, never again will they have a holiday equal to this."[32]

Imagining Jones's march as a threat to civil order, a line of police had formed to keep the marchers from entering Trenton, New Jersey, but they stepped aside when they saw the harmless bunch. People opened their doors to the children, offering them food and a place to stay. In Princeton the group settled into a barn for the evening. On hearing this, the owner of a fine local hotel drove out and offered them his lodging, free of charge.

Mother Jones was invited to speak to an economics class at nearby Princeton University the following morning. She brought ten-year-old James Ashworth with her. "Here's a textbook case in economics," she said, presenting the boy to the students and faculty. "He is stooped over because his spine is curved from carrying, day after day, bundles of yarn that weigh seventy-five pounds. He gets three dollars a week and his sister, who is fourteen, gets six dollars. They work in a carpet factory ten hours a day while the children of the rich are getting their higher education."[33] Moved by her words, Mother Jones's privileged audience clapped enthusiastically and took up a collection. Afterward they offered her a large donation. One student expressed shame for being from a wealthy family. "It's no sin to be rich, lad," she replied. "The sin is to gain your wealth from the sweat, toil, and privation of others."[34]

## Marchers Reach New York

The group continued on its way. Within a week they arrived in New York City, where cheering thousands turned out to welcome them at an evening rally. The Social Democratic Party offered them the use of its headquarters and the group remained in New York for a few days, giving speeches and drawing large crowds. Two days after their arrival, Mother Jones took the children to Coney Island to spend the day blissfully swimming in the surf and strolling the boardwalk. A circus owner named Frank Bostock invited the children to see his wild animal show, and offered the use of his facilities to Mother Jones.

*Children place caps on cans at a cannery. Jones's march to New York made the public aware of industry's widespread abuse of child workers.*

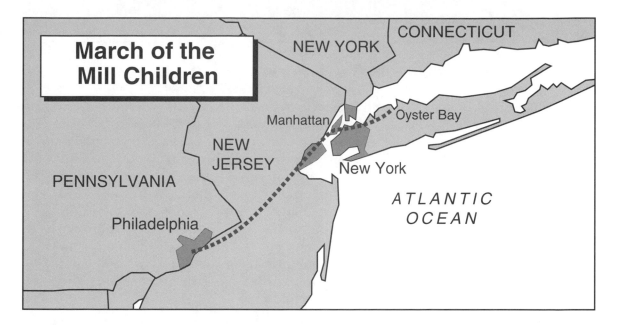

**March of the Mill Children**

That evening a large crowd filled the Bostock Building to hear her speak. "We are on our way to see President Roosevelt at Oyster Bay," she told them. "We will ask him to recommend the passage of a bill by Congress to protect children against the greed of the manufacturer." Then she added, "In Georgia, where children work day and night in the cotton mills, they have just passed a bill to protect song birds. What about the little children from whom all song is gone?"[35]

By then the marchers had been on the road nearly four weeks. Everyone was tired and more than ready for the last stage of the journey. Not wanting to overwhelm the president with too large a group, Mother Jones chose three children and four union representatives to accompany her to Oyster Bay. The rest of the group would remain in Manhattan, eagerly waiting to hear what the president had to say.

As it turned out, none of them would see Roosevelt. When the little group arrived at the president's mansion, they were stopped at the gates by his press secretary. The president "has nothing to do with child labor," Mr. William Barnes told the group. If Mother Jones wished, she was told, she could submit her comments "in writing."[36] But the president could not offer any help and he would not see them.

Undaunted, Jones returned to Manhattan with the children. She wrote to Roosevelt, telling him she would not leave New York City until she received an answer. She made arrangements to send the other marchers back to Philadelphia, but kept the three children with her, in case the president changed his mind. He did not. Jones got a message from Barnes a few days later, saying that the president sympathized with the children but was powerless to help them. The issue was up to Congress and the individual states.

After the anticipation and excitement of the long march, it was a deeply disappointing ending. Even if the president were truly powerless to help, his meeting with the group would have been a sym-

## "The Tears and Heartache of Little Children"

*Indifference to the suffering of the working class outraged Mother Jones. The following comments, from Irving Werstein's book* Labor's Defiant Lady, *are taken from a lecture she gave to a well-to-do New York audience.*

"You who live in comparative luxury! You whose children attend school, well-fed, well-clothed, well-shod. . . . You whose windows are adorned with fine lace curtains! Listen! Those fancy curtains hang between all of us and the future of the child who grows up in ignorance, body, mind, and soul dwarfed and diseased by relentless toil. . . . I declare that their little lives are entwined in the cotton goods they weave. That in the thread with which you sew your babies' clothes, the pure white confirmation dresses of your girls, their wedding gowns and dancing frocks, in that thread are twisted the tears and heartache of little children."

bolic victory: It would have sent the public the message that child labor reform was an important priority and emphasized its urgency. Federal legislation banning child labor would surely have been within reach. Now, instead, the children would simply return to the factories as usual. They might be changed inside by their glimpse of the wider world, but the deplorable conditions ruling their young lives would remain the same.

Even so, the march could not be called a failure. According to biographer Linda Atkinson, "Mary knew that the march had done a great deal of good. No one who had seen the children would ever forget them. And the children themselves were aware, as they had not been before, that what was happening to them was not fair, not natural. It did not happen to all children. The seeds of reform had been planted. Someday soon they would surely begin to grow."[37]

In terms of publicizing the problem of child labor, the march did succeed. Newspapers increased their coverage of child labor issues, raising public awareness and prompting people to pressure politicians and lawmakers to do something. The following year Pennsylvania drafted a law banning child labor. Although the law failed to get the full support it needed to pass, the issue had been brought before the voting public, a necessary first step on the road to child labor reform. By 1905 the existing Pennsylvania law was amended to require proof that a child was thirteen or older—and therefore legally able to work—other than his or her parents' signature on an affidavit.

The long, slow process of righting a terrible wrong had begun. Still, it would be thirty-six years before a federal law would prohibit child labor in the United States.

# Chapter

# 5 Warfare in West Virginia

Medieval West Virginia! With its tent colonies on the bleak hills! With its grim men and women! When I get to the other side, I shall tell God Almighty about West Virginia!

—Mother Jones,
*The Autobiography of Mother Jones*

"My address is like my shoes: it travels with me," Mother Jones once said. "I abide wherever there is a fight against wrong."[38] Mother Jones did indeed spend much of her life on the move, and the years from 1905 to 1911 were possibly her most restless ones. Her travels took her from the cotton mills of the deep South, to the Pennsylvania coalfields, to the Nebraska prairie, where she sold subscriptions and wrote a column for the *Appeal to Reason*, a socialist newspaper published in Omaha. During these busy years, she "formed her most radical associations,"[39] becoming an official lecturer for the Socialist Party, helping to found an international union (the Industrial Workers of the World, or IWW), and taking up the cause of Mexican revolutionaries seeking refuge in the United States. In 1910 she scored a big success when she helped young brewery workers in Milwaukee, Wisconsin, orga-

nize a union that freed them from low wages and poor working conditions.

Mother Jones spent the spring of 1912 on the West Coast and in the Pacific Northwest with striking railroad employees. Then it was on to Butte, Montana, where the copper miners were striking. She had begun preparing for a speaking tour of California to take place that summer when news from West Virginia began making the daily papers around the country.

*Jones spent most of her later years traveling throughout the United States, helping workers fight against low wages and unsafe working conditions.*

Apparently miners there were involved in a dispute with the coal companies and had gone on strike in April. Since then the situation had become increasingly violent. The trouble was in the Kanawha Valley, the very place Mother Jones had successfully organized, despite great opposition, ten years earlier. The union put in a request for Mother Jones to go to West Virginia as soon as possible to help the beleaguered strikers. "Now the battle had to be fought all over again," she wrote later. "I cancelled all my speaking dates in California, tied up all my possessions in a black shawl—I like travelling light—and went immediately to West Virginia."[40] What she found there appalled her. The coal miners and the company owners were locked in an armed struggle that more than anything else resembled a small-scale war.

## Return to Kanawha Valley

Together, the Paint Creek and Cabin Creek districts made up the Kanawha Valley. Relations between the two, which lay on either side of a steep ridge, had long been intertwined. Cabin Creek was unionized when Jones left the valley in 1902, but two years later the branch disintegrated and the company hired guards to keep the union and its organizers away from the miners. The union branch at Paint Creek was able to remain in place a few years longer, until the spring of 1912, when company owners refused to sign a renewal contract stating that the UMWA represented the miners. The union's response to this setback was to send in organizers to talk to the miners. The company, in turn, hired armed guards. Before long violence erupted.

The ensuing coal strike became, in short, one of the most violent disputes in American labor history. The coal company immediately turned the strikers out of their company-owned homes, so the UMWA set up temporary housing for the miners in a tent colony at a site called Holly Grove. Meanwhile the company imported strikebreakers from out of state to take the miners' jobs and hired hundreds of armed guards from West Virginia's Baldwin-Felts detective agency. Baldwin-Felts was notorious in those days for what Mother Jones called its "armed thugs." The agency provided coal companies with guards whose job it was to protect mine property.

## Mounting Violence

A camp was set up for the hired guards at Mucklow, not far from the miners' camp at Holly Grove, and machine guns were installed. The guards set to work, threatening, intimidating, and beating the striking miners and their family members. When beatings failed to discourage the miners, the guards turned to murder, with increasing frequency. The miners, in response, armed themselves, formed squadrons, and fought back. "If you haven't got good guns," Jones told them, "buy them."[41] Miners and guards attacked each other by turns, like armies at battle. The violence was intense.

Mother Jones appeared completely undaunted, regardless of the level of violence. She was determined to rally the workers. She went to work as usual, and continued to make her speeches encouraging the miners to persist in the strike.

*Jones speaks to a crowd in Kanawha Valley, where she rallied workers against the mining companies. Her fiery speeches aroused the attention of followers and critics alike.*

Her speeches during this time have been described as among the most inflammatory and militant of her career. Speaking to a crowd of six thousand gathered in Charleston, West Virginia, to protest the company's use of armed guards, she declared, "I am not going to say to you don't molest the [mine] operators. It is they who hire the dogs to shoot you. I am not asking you to do it; but if he is going to oppress you, deal with him."[42]

The company owners, public officials, and other influential people of the day criticized Mother Jones for her fiery exhortations. When she was on trial some weeks later for violating an injunction against public speaking, a prosecutor pointed at Mother Jones across the courtroom and declared, "There sits the most dangerous woman in America. She comes into a state where peace and progress reign. She crooks her finger—20,000 contented men lay down their tools and walk out."[43] Some contemporary scholars have added their voices to the charge that Mother Jones encouraged violence with her harsh words.

But on many other occasions Mother Jones spoke against violence and held the opinion she expressed once in a letter to a friend: "I am opposed to violence because violence only produces more violence and what is won today by violence will be lost tomorrow."[44] Mother Jones had strong feelings about the dire situation in West Virginia, however. The events there, dangerous as they were, demanded something other than her usual stance. Though she was basically opposed to promoting violence, Mother Jones at the same time felt, as she put it, that "when force is used to hinder the worker in his attempt to gain that which is his, he has the right to fight force with force."[45]

There was force in abundance in the Kanawha Valley. Violent clashes were a daily occurrence. On two occasions the governor declared martial law and sent the state militia into the strike areas to restore order. But when the governor withdrew the militia after several months, a number of the soldiers remained to accept jobs as private guards for the company, an arrangement that only increased

*Armed guards stand ready to defend against striking miners. The tension between the guards and the miners would quickly turn to bloody violence.*

the tension and hostility between strikers and guards in the area.

The strike, begun in April 1912, wore on into the following winter. The strikers' demands, which in the beginning had included a new contract with the union, higher pay, and payment in cash, not scrip, now included the removal of the brutal Baldwin-Felts guards. Removing the guards had, in fact, become the strikers' most urgent request. The company, for its part, steadfastly refused to meet any of the strikers' conditions.

Mother Jones continued to hold her emotion-charged meetings. She urged unorganized miners to join the union and used strong words to encourage those already on strike to keep fighting. Forbidden from being on company property, she needed to be cautious and very clever to do her work. She tried to avoid encounters with the armed guards, who seemed to be everywhere. On one occasion, company guards blocked her way as she hurried to a meeting, telling her she was on company property and could only proceed on public property. To do that, she would need to wade through a freezing cold creek. To their astonishment, no doubt, the white-haired old woman removed her shoes, hiked up her long skirt, and conducted her meeting from the middle of the frigid creek. Such devotion won the miners' hearts.

## Under Arrest

In early February 1913, without warning, the strike-related violence abruptly escalated into the bloodiest confrontations yet. One cold night, an armored car equipped with machine guns and carrying a load of company guards approached the strikers' tent colony at Holly Grove. The miners were sleeping peacefully in their tents when the guards opened fire on them. Miraculously, only one miner was killed while trying to flee his tent. Other men, women, and children were wounded as they slept in their beds. Enraged by the surprise attack on their sleeping camp, the miners marched a few days later to the guard camp at Mucklow. They surrounded the camp at night, and when the guards appeared in the morning, the miners opened fire. After a fierce gun battle lasting just minutes, thirteen guards lay dead. For the third time, the governor of West Virginia declared martial law and sent state troops to the strike areas.

This time the militia began a sweep, arresting strikers and organizers by the hundreds. Not a single company guard was arrested, however, or even disciplined,

## Dangerous Work

*The job of labor organizer was demanding and could be very dangerous. Organizing coal miners, which Mother Jones did for much of her life, was perhaps the most challenging work of all. According to labor historian Philip Foner, editor of* Mother Jones Speaks, *miners and organizers alike paid a high price for promoting change in the workplace.*

"Mining was not only the most grueling industry in which to labor but it was also the hardest for a union organizer. In no industry was the right to organize more bitterly fought, and union recognition . . . most often resulted only after hard, bloody battles between miners, company gunmen, coal and iron police, militiamen, and United States troops. The overwhelming power on the side of the mine operators led to the loss of many miners' lives as well as strikes. Union organizers also paid with their lives. There were coal regions union organizers did not dare enter, for it was certain they would never leave alive."

*Organizing coal miners into a union was challenging, dangerous work.*

an apparent bias that prompted Mother Jones to organize a trip to Charleston, the state capital, to protest to the governor. A group of miners would accompany her: They planned to tell their side of the story to the governor and see what he might do. Little did they know that a wild rumor preceded them: Mother Jones was supposedly on her way to Charleston with an army of 3,500 to kill the governor and blow up the capitol building.

The militia was ready and waiting for the protesters. As soon as they stepped off the train in Charleston, Mother Jones and the miners, a group of no more than thirty-five, were arrested, reboarded, transported to Kanawha Valley military headquarters in Pratt, West Virginia, and booked into jail. Mother Jones was charged with stealing a machine gun, attempting to blow up a train with dynamite, and conspiracy to murder, a charge punishable by death. Although they were civilians arrested in a civilian zone, and not in an area that was under martial law, Mother Jones and the miners were informed that they would have to face a military tribunal rather than the standard trial by jury in a civil court.

The eighty-three-year-old woman was put into solitary confinement to await her trial. In a letter to her old friend Terrence Powderly, Mother Jones wrote, "My dear friend, you have no doubt heard of my arrest by the hounds of capital pirates. They have me in close confinement. There are 2 military guarding me day and night. No one is allowed to speak to me."[46] Twenty-two days after Mother Jones's arrest, a military trial took place, but the verdict was kept secret.

Meanwhile, the new governor of West Virginia, Henry Hatfield, came to the Kanawha Valley to see for himself the area that was causing all the trouble. After meeting with various people and touring the district, he went to the "little shack" where Mary was being guarded. There he found her "lying on a straw tick on the floor, carrying a temperature of 104, very rapid respiration, and a constant cough."[47] A doctor confirmed that Mother Jones had pneumonia.

Imprisoning an elderly woman was in itself an unpopular step, the governor knew. He could not risk the public's finding out that Mother Jones was not only in jail but seriously ill as well. That news would certainly upset the many admirers

*When Governor Henry Hatfield arrived in the Kanawha Valley, he found Jones in jail and suffering from pneumonia. He secretly arranged to have her sent to a hospital until she regained her strength.*

Jones had around the country, and focus considerable attention on the Kanawha Valley, where events were steadily worsening. Governor Hatfield arranged for Mother Jones to be sent secretly to a hospital in Charleston. When she regained her strength, she would be returned to solitary confinement.

## Widespread Publicity

Despite the governor's secrecy, word of these events leaked out. A writer for *Collier's Magazine* wrote a long story informing the public about Mother Jones's imprisonment and her illness. Predictably, the public was outraged. People began demanding Jones's immediate release and information about what was going on in West Virginia. Word spread of the atrocities being committed against miners and their families there. Calls went out for a congressional investigation into the dispute between the company and miners. At last, the strike was getting widespread and much-needed publicity. Locked behind the doors of a military prison, Mother Jones still managed to do the one thing that could help the miners most: She had gotten the attention of the entire nation.

A senator from Indiana to whom Mother Jones had appealed in her letters put the issue before his colleagues. Congress must send a special committee to West Virginia, he insisted, to investigate the "reign of terror" there. A senator representing West Virginia protested loudly, arguing that the mine owners, having "conquered the wilderness,"[48] were entitled to the protection of the government. As for Mother Jones, he claimed, she

caused riots. The other senators, though, could see that the situation in West Virginia had to be investigated. Hearing of Mother Jones's imprisonment and details of the fighting between miners and guards convinced them that something was definitely wrong in the Kanawha Valley. Within a week, a congressional committee was on its way to West Virginia.

In the end, the mining companies were forced to negotiate with the union and to agree to some of the miners' demands. The workday was reduced to nine hours. Miners were allowed the right to make purchases at places other than the company store. The UMWA won recognition as the official representative of the miners, a crucial victory. The governor guaranteed that in the future, citizens had the right to be tried in civil, not military, courts. And finally, the governor announced what many had been waiting to hear: Mother Jones and the others imprisoned by the military were to be released. After nearly three months of solitary confinement, Mother Jones's sentence—revealed to be twenty years in prison—was commuted, and she was freed.

## "A More Highly Developed Citizenship"

The victory was an important one for Mother Jones. A few days after her release, she gave a speech at Carnegie Hall in New York City to a packed audience. "Mother Jones Stirs Crowd," announced the headline in the *New York Times*. According to another newspaper, she was received with "shouting, stamping, and handclapping" and "women surged down

## "From out of These Prison Walls"

*While in prison, Mother Jones smuggled out a telegram to Senator John W. Kern of Indiana, The telegram is taken from* Mother Jones: Labor Crusader.

"From out of the military prison wall of Pratt, West Virginia, where I have walked over my eighty-fourth milestone in history, I send you the groans and tears and heartaches of men, women and children as I have heard them in this state. From out of these prison walls, I plead with you for the honor of the nation, to push that investigation, and the children yet unborn will rise and call you blessed."

the aisles toward the stage and threw kisses to the aged agitator and flowers at her feet."[49] Standing before the cheering, enthusiastic audience, Mother Jones reminisced about her experiences in the Kanawha Valley. The violent clashes there and Jones's fiery speeches to the miners had both been well publicized in recent months, and she seemed to have her critics in mind as she spoke to the crowd:

Men, women, and children were evicted from their homes; miners were shot down in cold blood, and the reign of terror grew even more terrible. When I protested the barbarism of the capitalists and their henchmen, I was deprived of all the rights of an American citizen and imprisoned in a military bastile for three months. . . . I am in favor of using the ballot, and in all my career I have never advocated violence. What I want to do is to give the nation a more highly developed citizenship.[50]

When she left West Virginia this time, Mother Jones was eighty-three years old, well beyond the age when most people have retired from their life's work. She had laurels to rest on and might have been expected to seek the time and calm to reflect on her accomplishments. But Jones was not ready for rest. Her good health restored, she had an energy and drive uncommon in a woman half her age. Her plans did not include sitting still, at least for long. As she saw it, there was still work to do. And in fact, the toughest strike she would ever get involved in was just around the corner.

# 6 Back to Colorado

They went out on the black mountain sides, lived in tents through a horrible winter with eighteen inches of snow on the ground. They tied their feet in gunny sacks and lived lean and lank and hungry as timber wolves.

—Mother Jones,
*The Autobiography of Mother Jones*

After her success in West Virginia, Mother Jones traveled to Washington, D.C., to visit Terrence and Emma Powderly, her close friends of many years. The Powderlys had an extra room in their home where they often hosted their friends in the labor movement, and they tried to talk Mother Jones into settling there and living with them. Mother Jones had not had so much as a room to call her own in many years. The Powderlys' offer would enable her to retire from her grueling schedule, to bring to a close her remarkable career, and to live among friends, of whom she had many in the area.

It was a generous offer and it must have been tempting, but Mother Jones could not be persuaded to accept. She simply was not ready to stop working. She spent the summer of 1913 with the Powderlys, but by late August she was back on the road. On Labor Day she was in Texas on a speaking tour. Not long after, the UMWA was calling on her again: There were labor troubles in Colorado and her help was needed.

## North and South Divide

For ages, it seemed, the UMWA had been trying to make inroads into the troubled coalfields of Colorado. In 1903 Mother Jones had been trying to organize workers in the southern part of the state, but her efforts got her into trouble with the president of the UMWA, John Mitchell. At the time, miners in both northern and southern Colorado were on strike. The northerners were told by the company that if they quit striking and returned to work, they would gain several of their union demands. Jones felt strongly, however, that the miners were more powerful if they all stayed together, and that the northerners should not return to work until their fellow workers in the south, who were even more poorly treated, were also promised concessions. When Mitchell insisted over Mother Jones's objections that the northerners accept terms and end the strike, she was bitterly angry with him. When production resumed in the north there was no further coal shortage, and the com-

*A bleak mining town sits among the hills. Even years after Jones began her work, miserable working conditions still existed in some areas.*

pany felt no pressure to listen to the southern workers, who, in effect, had been abandoned by the union. Mother Jones never forgave Mitchell.

Eventually, the northern Colorado miners lost the gains they had made, just as Mother Jones had predicted they would, and soon the entire state was in need of union assistance again. This time the union, under the leadership of a new president, was determined to make progress in the southern field as well, where the company remained especially hostile to the union. In the spring of 1913 the UMWA initiated a campaign to challenge the company and began calling in its best organizers for the dangerous job. Organizers went to work in Colorado through the summer, many of them in the Trinidad area, where the situation was especially volatile. In mid-September, Mother Jones arrived.

## Miners' Bleak Existence

Little had changed for the miners since Mother Jones had been in the state ten years earlier. The miserable living and working conditions that prevailed in 1903 remained substantially the same. Industrialist John D. Rockefeller's powerful Colorado Fuel and Iron Company ran twenty-seven mining camps and produced 40 percent of the state's coal. The CF & I controlled the smallest details of the miners' lives, including determining where the men and their families could buy food and other necessities. According to one of the mining company's own investigators, the company-built houses where the miners lived were among "the most repulsive looking rat-holes to be found anywhere in America." He described them as "hovels, shacks and dugouts unfit for the habitation of human beings."[51] Labor historians offer similarly bleak descriptions:

> No words can adequately describe the contrast between the wild beauty of the Colorado countryside and the unspeakable squalor of these mining camps. The miners' huts, which were usually shared by several families, were made up of clapboard walls and thin-planked floors, with leaking roofs, sagging doors, broken windows, and old newspapers nailed to the walls to keep out the cold. Some families, particularly the black families, were forced to live in tiny cubicles not much larger than chicken coops.[52]

These poor housing and sanitation conditions were to blame for outbreaks of typhoid fever among workers and their families, 151 cases in one year alone.

The miners' working environment was no better than their living arrangements. The job of mining coal was always hazardous, but in 1912 workers in Colorado were killed in mining accidents at a rate double the national average. The long working days—ten to twelve hours, six days a week—exhausted the miners. Wages already too low were driven down even further by common company practices that cheated workers. As in West Virginia, miners were paid according to the amount of coal they dug, and the company likewise underreported the coal's true weight. Though a Colorado state law prohibited paying the workers in scrip, mine operators continued the practice, forcing poor families to rely on the overpriced company stores. The mining companies were so powerful that they could break laws without fear of consequences.

## Ten Thousand Strikers

The UMWA finally called a statewide strike to protest these conditions. On September 23, 1913, in a cold, driving rain,

*An inspector weighs a load of coal just mined by workers. A common company practice was to underreport the true weight of the coal to cheat workers who were paid by the amount of coal they dug.*

ten thousand miners—nearly all the miners in the southern district—moved out of their company-owned houses under the watchful eyes and rifles of company guards, and into tent colonies provided by the union. The company had prepared for the strike, buying loads of ammunition, hiring numerous Baldwin-Felts guards and detectives, and constructing "The Death Special," an armored car equipped with a machine gun capable of firing four hundred rounds a minute. This threatening presence patrolled the valley daily, cruising slowly past the tent colonies where the miners and their families stayed. The miners, in turn, obtained whatever weapons they could, stashing rifles and shotguns alongside the bedrolls in their flimsy tents.

Before the sun had set on the opening day of the strike, the first miners had lost their lives. The violence increased in the coming weeks, but the miners stayed with the strike, encouraged by Mother Jones's speeches and the support of the union. When miners went on strike, coal lay unmined in the ground and the company began to lose money. Striking was the one sure way miners could make the company pay attention to their concerns.

The governor of Colorado, Elias Ammons, began feeling pressure to do something about the potentially explosive situation in Trinidad. After visiting the strike area, he ordered the state militia in to keep the peace, but it soon became clear that the soldiers had no intention of protecting the striking miners. Just as the militia had done in West Virginia, the Colorado state militia sided with the coal company. The soldiers threatened the miners, broke up their meetings, and attacked and beat the miners and their wives and children. The commander of

the militia, Brigadier General John Chase, traveled around the area in a CF & I company car with no pretense of mediating the conflict and unconcerned, apparently, by the impression he made. With the arrival of the state militia, the company now had what amounted to its own private army.

Alarmed by this ominous turn of events, Mother Jones traveled to Denver, the state capital, to protest the military's presence in Trinidad. An annual union meeting was under way in Denver and she recruited two thousand union members to join her in a protest march to the capitol building. There the group voiced their concerns to Governor Ammons, calling for a stop to the threats and brutality being carried out in Trinidad by the militia and company guards. They requested that General Chase be removed from the strike

*When tensions mounted during the Trinidad, Colorado, strike, Governor Elias Ammons sent in the state militia.*

zone and the machine guns taken away. The governor, who feared the power of the mining companies, informed the crowd that before he could take any action in Trinidad he needed to see a report listing names and places as proof of the charges against the coal company and the militia. The union members should form a committee, he advised, and submit a list of grievances to him.

While a committee was being formed and set to this task, the miners were enduring the worst Colorado winter in thirty years. The UMWA, meanwhile, sent Mother Jones to El Paso, Texas, where the union had learned the CF & I was luring Mexican immigrants across the Texas border with promises of good jobs, then transporting them to Colorado to work as strikebreakers in the mines. When the Mexican workers arrived and learned the truth about their jobs, they were stuck, prevented from leaving by the militia. Despite the strike, the company was getting the workers it needed and production had barely slowed. Mother Jones went to El Paso to put a stop to the practice. She made public speeches warning people not to believe false promises about high wages and good jobs. She explained that the work was temporary, low paying, and hazardous. By accepting such work, she argued, the immigrants would not only harm the strikers' cause but also put themselves in the middle of a violent strike zone, thereby endangering themselves.

## Warning from Trinidad

In Trinidad, meanwhile, General Chase had a few words to say about Mother

*Fearing that Jones would incite the strikers, Brigadier General John Chase warned Jones that she would be arrested if she came to Trinidad.*

Jones. "She will be jailed immediately if she comes to Trinidad," he warned. "I am not going to give her a chance to make any more speeches here. She is dangerous because she inflames the minds of the strikers."[53] Such warnings never deterred Mother Jones. When informed of his intentions, she told reporters, "Tell General Chase that Mother Jones is going to Trinidad in a day or two and that he'd better play his strongest cards—the militia's guns—against her."[54]

When she arrived in Trinidad a few days later, Mother Jones was immediately arrested and given a military escort out of town, just as the general had promised. As she was put on a train for Denver, she called out that she would be back "when Colorado is made part of the United States."[55] She spent the next several days in Denver, meeting with union officials and buying supplies for the strikers, including $500 worth of shoes for miners' families. Then, undetected by military police posted at railroad stations throughout the state, Mother Jones made her way back to Trinidad.

Back in Trinidad for only half a day before General Chase learned of her presence, Jones was again arrested, and placed under military confinement at the San Rafael Hospital on the outskirts of Trinidad, where she was assigned to a hospital room. A guard was stationed at her door, twenty-four hours a day, to prevent her from leaving. No charges were filed against her and no trial date was scheduled, although holding her without doing both of these things violated the U.S. Constitution. The UMWA immediately filed a petition demanding her release. Hundreds of women—the wives, mothers, and sisters of miners—organized a march down Trinidad's main street protesting the arrest. Governor Ammons and General Chase ignored them all.

The injustices being committed in Colorado were no longer going unnoticed, however. Mother Jones's unlawful imprisonment, once public knowledge, initiated a wave of sympathy nationwide. Congress announced that it was launching an immediate investigation into the Colorado strike. When, as part of this investigation, a congressional committee arrived in Trinidad, Mother Jones was suddenly released from her guarded room, eight weeks after she had been arrested. At Governor Ammons's request, she was put on a train and brought to Denver.

The governor, like General Chase, claimed that Mother Jones's speeches to the miners contributed to the strike-related violence. At a meeting in his office, he told Mother Jones that she would be arrested again if she returned to Trinidad, or anywhere within the strike zone for that matter. He asked her to promise to stay away. Mother Jones refused, of course, to make any such promises. The strike zone was dangerous, the governor insisted, no place for an old woman. He warned her to follow his advice.

"Governor," Mother Jones replied, "if Washington took instructions from such as you, we would be under King George's descendants yet! If Lincoln took instructions from you, Grant would never have gone to Gettysburg. I think I had better not take your orders."[56] And with that, she left his office.

## Behind Bars Again

Mother Jones spent the next few days in Denver, then once more boarded a train for Trinidad. At 5:30 A.M., in Walsenburg, a small town shy of its destination, the train was stopped and boarded by soldiers. They searched the cars for Mother Jones, and when they found her they arrested her and brought her to the Walsenburg County Courthouse. On this her third arrest, she was taken to a basement jail cell and locked up. Once again, no charges were filed, no trial date was set. She was simply ordered held until further notice.

It was a cold, terrible place, without heat, damp and dark," Mother Jones wrote later. "I slept in my clothes by day, and at night I fought great sewer rats with a beer bottle. 'If I were out of this dungeon,' thought I, 'I would be fighting the human sewer rats anyway!'"[57] She spent her time looking out the basement window at the shoes passing on the street outside, sometimes talking with the children who bent to look in before the guards shooed them away.

Mother Jones's third arrest and harshest imprisonment to date succeeded in raising enormous public outcry and sympathy, both for herself and for the striking miners. Telegrams demanding her release flooded the governor's office and the White House. "Has it come to this, that men so fear the truth that they must unlawfully imprison and silence this woman of eighty-two years?" asked James Brewster, a University of Colorado law professor and member of a committee making recommendations to Governor Ammons. Later, testifying before a federal commission, Brewster declared that the arrest of Mother Jones, "without a warrant, without any suspicion of crime, was one of the greatest outrages upon civilized American jurisdiction that has been perpetrated."[58]

## Testimony Before Congress

Mother Jones was held illegally in her dungeonlike cell for nearly a month.

### Letter from Prison

*A letter Mother Jones wrote while imprisoned in a rat-infested basement cell was smuggled past security guards and appeared in newspapers across the country the following day. Excerpted here from Fetherling's* The Miners' Angel, *the letter helped to raise public awareness about the miners' struggle.*

"I have discovered what appears to be an opportunity to smuggle a letter out of prison and shall attempt to get this communication by the armed guards which day and night surround me. . . . I want to say to the public that I am an American citizen. I have never broken a law in my life and I claim the right of an American citizen to go where I please so long as I do not violate the law. . . . I ask the press to let the nation know of my treatment and to say to my friends . . . that not even my incarceration in a damp underground dungeon will make me give up the fight in which I am engaged for liberty and for the rights of the working people. Of course I long to be out of prison. To be shut from the sunlight is not pleasant but . . . I shall stand firm. To be in prison is no disgrace. . . . Let the nation know . . . that the Great United States of America . . . is now holding Mother Jones incommunicado in an underground cell surrounded by rats, tin horn soldiers and other vermin."

Then, as before, she was abruptly released. As soon as she was free, she traveled to Washington, D.C., to testify before the House Mines and Mining Committee, which had recently resumed hearings, in part because of publicity surrounding her imprisonment. John D. Rockefeller Jr., heir to the CF & I fortune, had already testified before the committee. Rockefeller, a handsome and articulate man used to charming his opponents, spoke of his opposition to the union and his willingness to spend large sums of money to keep it out. "I have been so greatly interested in the matter, and have such a warm sympathy for this

*Testifying before the House Mines and Mining Committee, John D. Rockefeller Jr., heir to the Colorado Fuel and Iron Company, dubiously claimed to support the miners.*

very large number of men who work for us," Rockefeller said, "that I should be the last to surrender the liberty under which they have been working and the conditions which to them have been entirely satisfactory, to give up that liberty and accept dictation from those outside who have no interest in them or the company."[59]

But the committee found Rockefeller's statements of concern for the miners dubious at best. When they questioned him further, they learned that Rockefeller had not visited the Colorado coal camps in ten years. He had not even been to a Colorado Fuel and Iron Company meeting in the past decade, though he had been put in charge of his father's properties there. Rockefeller might claim to be interested in the miners and fighting for their freedom, but the evidence said otherwise.

Mother Jones took the witness stand after Rockefeller. She spoke urgently about the conflict in Colorado and the abuses of power by the militia. She told of the beatings and murders strikers suffered at the hands of the guards. The guards, she testified, were "permitted to arm themselves with machine guns and use them on the workers, because the ruling class wants quick results."[60] She urged the committee to get involved and take measures to intervene on the strikers' behalf. One of the committee members read aloud excerpts from Mother Jones's inflammatory West Virginia speeches and asked whether she had said or done anything to provoke the violence in Colorado. Mother Jones sharply denied the suggestion, invoking the name of a deeply respected leader who had also known violent turmoil. "That is not half as radical as Lincoln," she replied. "I have heard him make a great deal more radical speech."[61]

*A 1914 photo shows a slain Colorado miner, one of the casualties of the Ludlow Massacre.*

## The Ludlow Massacre

Mother Jones's testimony created a surge of public support for the strikers. Afterwards, she remained in Washington, D.C., for a few days to spend time with the Powderlys. Meanwhile, in the spring of 1914 in the Colorado mountains, tensions continued to simmer. There was a brief respite from the fighting on April 19, the date when the miners of Greek ancestry celebrated Easter. In the tent colony at Ludlow, the immigrant families had a holiday. They feasted on Greek dishes, played games, danced, and sang. Distracted for a few hours from their troubles, the families shared a happy and festive evening together.

But with sunrise the following morning, fear spread quickly through the camp. Two companies of soldiers stationed on a nearby hillside had begun practice drilling with their guns. Word went out among the miners that everyone was to get up, get dressed, and be prepared to defend themselves. Suddenly, two militia-fired bombs burst in the skies over the miners' camp, signaling that an attack was imminent. Weapons in hand, the miners spread out over the grounds, taking their places in defense.

*Smoke engulfs a miners' camp, set on fire during the battle between miners and Colorado mining companies.*

Journalist and war correspondent John Reed was on hand to witness what occurred next. "Suddenly," Reed reported, "the machine guns pounded stab-stab-stab full on the tents. The most awful panic followed. Some of the women and children streamed out over the plain, to get away from the tent colony. They were shot as they ran."[62] Others sought safety by crawling down into pits that had been dug beneath the tents for just such an emergency. A young boy who ran back to his tent for his pet kitten was shot and killed. The troops had ceased "to be an army and had become a mob,"[63] shooting at anything that moved, repeatedly spraying the tents with machine-gun fire. Many of the women and children fled to safety in the hills around Ludlow. Others remained hiding in the tent colony. The miners returned fire all day, but they were no match for the militia. Late in the afternoon, a UMWA official emerged from a tent, carrying the white flag of surrender. He was shot dead.

After driving more of the miners into the hills, the soldiers rampaged through the colony, looting the tents for anything of value. Then they set the tents on fire, and soon, roaring flames consumed what little remained of the colony at Ludlow. The next morning, when the fire had subsided and the soldiers were gone, the miners and their families came down out of the hills and returned to the devastated camp. They picked through charred pots and pans, burned clothing, bullet-ridden baby carriages and toys. To their horror, they discovered in a pit beneath one of the tents, where they had crawled seeking safety, the burned bodies of eleven children and two young mothers. At least twice as many more bodies of miners were found among the debris.

The company guards had finally pushed the strikers too far. In fury, the miners grabbed their weapons and fought back, destroying and setting fire to company properties for two hundred miles around. Joined by many Colorado citizens who shared their anger at the massacre, the miners rioted for ten days, demolishing property and attacking and driving out any soldiers who tried to stop them.

When word of the brutal massacre at Ludlow spread, the rest of the nation was shocked and outraged, too. Showing their support for the miners, people staged protests in cities around the country from San Francisco to New York. "There were several days when there was a positive danger of a national revolution growing out of this Colorado strike,"[64] concluded a

## Massacre at Ludlow

*In the spring of 1915 a government committee began an investigation into the Colorado strike of 1913–14. Many people were called to testify, including the Petruccis, a miner and his wife whose three children died in the Ludlow Massacre on April 20, 1914. This excerpt is from Mary Petrucci's testimony, quoted in* Where the Sun Never Shines.

"You're not to think we could do any differently another time. We are working people—my husband and I—and we're stronger for the union than before the strike. . . . I can't have my babies back. But perhaps when everybody knows about them, something will be done to make the world a better place for all babies."

*A group of reporters takes cover under a truce flag, while dead bodies are removed from the Ludlow mining camp.*

government report written later. President Woodrow Wilson had to send the U.S. Army to Colorado to stop the violence. Only with the arrival of federal troops did Governor Ammons finally withdraw the Colorado state militia, halt the importation of strikebreakers, and put a stop to the bloodshed.

In Denver a crowd of five thousand gathered on the grounds of the state capitol to listen to various speakers, including a journalist who denounced the governor and Rockefeller as "accessories to the murder of babes."[65] Mother Jones, devastated by the tragedy, arrived in the middle of the rally, on her return from Washington, D.C. "She took off her bonnet and threw up a clenched fist in welcome" and the crowd roared its approval. "Here I am again, boys, just back from Washington," she told those assembled, "and you aren't licked by a whole lot. Washington is aroused and there is help coming." Then she added, "We'll make some laws to put the Colorado Fuel & Iron Company out of business and Mr. Rockefeller too."[66]

## No Settlement

Although the violence had been stopped, the strike dragged on into the summer of 1914. President Wilson appointed a committee to draw up a settlement aimed at pleasing both sides of the conflict. Mother Jones, meanwhile, embarked on a national speaking tour to raise money and support for the strikers' cause. When the president's committee revealed their proposal, a moderate set of conditions granting each side a few concessions, the miners, though they had hoped for more, voted to accept the terms. The coal companies, however, arrogantly rejected the settlement outright.

Still fighting for the miners, Mother Jones returned to Washington to speak to Congress and to see President Wilson again. She urged the president to take control of the coal mines out of the hands of the coal companies and to authorize the government to run the mines instead. "No operator, no coal company on the face of the earth made that coal," she argued. "It

*A settlement committee appointed by President Wilson listens to Governor Ammons speak before presenting its proposal. The coal companies flatly refused the settlement, which granted concessions to both strikers and the companies.*

## "Men's Hearts Are Cold"

*Mother Jones, remembering the Colorado defeat years later in her autobiography, wrote eloquently about the hard life of the miner.*

"Men's hearts are cold. They are indifferent. Not all the coal that is dug warms the world. It remains indifferent to the lives of those who risk their life and health down in the blackness of the earth; who crawl through dark, choking crevices with only a bit of a lamp on their caps to light their silent way; whose backs are bent with toil, whose very bones ache, whose happiness is sleep, and whose peace is death."

is a mineral; it belongs to the nation; it was there down the ages, and it belongs to every generation that comes along."[67] Although President Wilson had no intention of authorizing the government to run the coal industry, he did set up another settlement committee, and he emphasized that his sympathies were with the miners.

But sympathy was not enough. Despite public outcry over the events in Colorado, the efforts of Mother Jones and other union officials, even the intervention of the president, the coal companies adamantly refused to negotiate and there were as yet no laws in place to force them to do so. Having no other option, the UMWA ended the strike in December of 1914 and the miners returned to work. They went back on the company's terms, to the same oppressive, unfair conditions that existed before the strike and all its subsequent turmoil.

The Colorado Fuel & Iron strike of 1913–14 is remembered today as "one of the most grueling, long-lasting, and widely known industrial conflicts in the history of the U.S."[68] The outcome of the conflict bitterly disappointed Mother Jones. Speaking to a crowd of thousands in New York's Cooper Union a month after the defeat, she was uncharacteristically grim. The union lost in Colorado, she said, because on their side the workers "had only the Constitution. The other side had bayonets. In the end, bayonets always win."[69]

Ultimately, the union would prevail in Colorado, but not for several more years. Like West Virginia, Colorado would not be fully unionized until 1933. A few years later, the federal government would pass the National Industrial Recovery Act and the Fair Labor Standards Act, laws that, among other things, guaranteed the union's right to represent workers in every state. But that day was yet to come. In the meantime, Mother Jones was growing old. She was now well into her eighties, an old woman embarked on her final years.

# 7 "The Future is in Labor's Strong, Rough Hands"

The future is in labor's strong, rough hands.

—Mother Jones,
*The Autobiography of Mother Jones*

Mother Jones was facing yet another courtroom trial, the final one of her long life. The year was 1919 and she had become embroiled in a steel strike in the small Pennsylvania town of Homestead, where twenty-five years earlier a famous labor conflict, the "Battle of Homestead," had been fought. In that brutal crackdown on striking steelworkers, a dozen workers lost their lives, hundreds were injured, and thousands were blacklisted, ever after prevented from working in the steel industry. Now the union was attempting once again to organize the Homestead region, as well as other areas of Pennsylvania. Mother Jones had recently arrived to help.

Two days before, Jones had spoken at a workers' rally held at the site of the former bloodshed. In the middle of her speech, she was arrested, charged with violating the injunctions against public speaking, and ordered to appear in court.

*At the age of eighty-nine, Jones was arrested for the last time at a workers' rally in Pennsylvania.*

*A labor organization gathers in the street in 1914. After the failure of the Colorado strike, Jones continued to travel throughout the country, joining strikers and offering her assistance where needed.*

Seated now before a "cranky old judge," Mother Jones was on trial, answering a series of questions. The judge wanted to know if she had a permit to speak on the streets. "Yes, sir," she told him, "I had a permit." And who, the judge asked, had issued it? "Patrick Henry, Thomas Jefferson, and John Adams!"[70] Mother Jones replied.

The judge was not amused by her clever joke. He imposed a heavy fine, but then let the elderly woman go. She was, after all, in her late eighties. Even so, Mother Jones had not yet retired. She was still living much as she had in her younger years, ferociously defending the workers and speaking out on their behalf at every opportunity. Conflict still attracted her, as it always had, and she had not lost the special ability she seemed to have for putting herself in the middle of one.

After the failed coal strike of 1913–14, Mother Jones maintained her trademark strenuous pace for the next few years, for much of that time on the move.

She remained focused on labor battles, crisscrossing the country from the scene of one strike to another, offering her assistance and boosting the striking workers' morale with her encouragement and enthusiasm. In 1915 she organized streetcar workers in New York City. The following year she joined garment district workers on strike in Chicago.

World War I had begun in Europe in 1914. As did many of her friends, Mother Jones opposed the war. Though she declined to participate in antiwar demonstrations held around the country to protest American involvement in the conflict, she was not reluctant to express her

## Good Health and a Long Life

*During her eighties and nineties, Mother Jones continued to work and to travel. In the following interview excerpt, from* Mother Jones Speaks, *Jones, eighty-three at the time, talks with a newspaper reporter about aging.*

"I attribute my good health and unimpaired faculties to the life of activity which I have led. Many people retire from active life at the age of 50 and spend the rest of their years in peace and quietness. They allow their mental faculties to become dulled by not exercising them, and by not continuing to take an interest in affairs. I was nearly fifty when I took up the business of agitating to improve labor conditions. My mind is kept constantly on the alert coping with difficulties, planning campaigns, organizing work along new lines and with striving to better present-day conditions. I have no time to think about getting old; besides I have a lot to accomplish yet."

disapproval. In 1917 she was asked to help defend Tom Mooney, a well-known socialist. Mooney was also a pacifist and an outspoken opponent of the war, and for his views was considered by the U.S. government to be a dangerous radical. When a bomb exploded at an antiwar protest, Mooney was charged with the crime and sentenced to death by hanging, though there was evidence he was not even at the scene when the explosion occurred. Mother Jones took the unpopular stand of supporting Mooney, touring the West Coast to make speeches on his behalf and to raise money for his defense. In part through her efforts, Mooney's life was spared at the last minute when his sentence was changed from hanging to life imprisonment. Twenty-two years later, when it was finally revealed he had been framed, he was pardoned and freed.

Mother Jones stirred controversy again in 1920 when, to the dismay and disappointment of many women, she publicly opposed the just-passed Nineteenth Amendment to the Constitution, which gave women the right to vote. "I have never had a vote and I have raised hell all over this country," she told a group of suffragettes. "You don't need a vote to raise hell. You need convictions and a voice!"[71] She made similar comments to the press, adding that she believed women should stay at home with their children. "In no sense of the word am I in favor of women's suffrage," she commented. "Women already have a great responsibility on their shoulders. Home training of the child should be their task, and it is the most beautiful of tasks."[72] She repeated such sentiments often in the following years, never passing up an opportunity to make them public.

Such traditional, old-fashioned attitudes, voiced often in the early days of the women's movement, nevertheless sounded astonishing coming from the mouth of Mother Jones. As biographer Linda Atkinson observes, "It was strange to hear this view from a woman who had lived a decidely 'public' life, who had urged women to join their husbands on picket lines, who had unionized working women, who had in fact done her best to change an entire culture—and who had not had a home, or even a permanent address, for over fifty years."[73] Mother Jones's conservative views were all the more puzzling because in previous years she had often spoken out in support of women's role in public life. At the UMWA's annual convention in 1901, for example, she gave a speech urging women to participate in the union:

My friends, it is often asked, "Why should a woman be out talking about miners' affairs?" Why shouldn't she? Who has a better right? Has she not given you birth? Has she not raised you and cared for you? Has she not struggled along for you?[74]

Mother Jones's later words opposing women's rights did not square with her actions. All her life she had been an independent, outspoken, and strong-willed woman—an unlikely candidate for her own advice about staying at home out of the way. She had often relied on the support of women to turn strikes around, using them to rally the strikers or to confront the strikebreakers, as they had in

*Women from around the country prepare to march on Washington as part of the fight for women's suffrage. When Congress passed the Nineteenth Amendment, giving women the right to vote, Jones, to the surprise of many, voiced her opposition.*

the "mop and broom brigade" incident at Coal Creek. Why she felt strongly about "women's place," or why she would deny women the fundamental right to vote, was something of a mystery.

Mother Jones often said she objected to the suffragettes because theirs was a "middle-class" movement. It was true that the women working for suffrage were not the wives and daughters of coal miners; they were far more likely to be related to bankers or lawyers or other professionals. Jones believed the suffragettes' life experiences left them unaware of the problems working people faced and unconcerned about solving them. Coming from a working-class background herself, Mother Jones had long felt estranged from the middle class. She was suspicious of its bureaucratic methods and uncomfortable with its formalities and resistance to change. She disliked organizations. Her lifelong distrust of politicans, lawyers, preachers, and authority of any sort extended to include even labor leaders.

Even if women had the vote, Mother Jones argued, it would not make a difference in the workers' lives. "The women of Colorado have had the vote for two generations and the working men and women are in slavery," she said, referring to working conditions in such places as Trinidad, Colorado. "What good is the ballot, if they don't use it?"[75] For Mother Jones, the working-class struggle was always more important than the women's rights movement.

## A Proponent of Socialism

Regardless of the issue, it simply was not unusual for Mother Jones to do or say things that appeared contradictory or that offended some. Labor historians and biographers refer repeatedly to what they see as inconsistencies in her speech and behavior. She was a powerful woman in a nontraditional role, but she opposed legally empowering women with the vote. She claimed to be against violence, but many believe she encouraged violence by urging miners to buy guns and by making inflammatory speeches. At one time or another, she clashed with all of her colleagues, most intensely with those in positions of institutional authority and power, such as John Mitchell, president of the UMWA.

"Mother Jones was always doubtful of the good of organized institutions," the famous trial attorney Clarence Darrow wrote in his foreword to her autobiography. "These require compromises and she could not compromise. To her there was but one side. Right and wrong were forever distinct."[76] Indeed, Mother Jones's most vocal criticism of John Mitchell was that he accepted compromises to settle labor disputes. The way she saw it, he was abandoning the workers.

John Mitchell and Mother Jones had very different ideas about the best way to help the workers. Their opposing attitudes toward a growing split within the UMWA illustrate the difference in their personal philosophies. While Mitchell sided with those in the union who favored "pure and simple" unionism, Jones counted herself with those union members who embraced socialist ideals. The "pure and simple" unionists were pragmatists, or practical thinkers, who had a single goal: to achieve better working conditions, including higher wages, for the workers. Their attitude was mainstream and eventually it pre-

## "Simply a Social Revolutionist"

*A lifelong advocate of socialist principles, Mother Jones was for a time a member of the Socialist Party in the United States. She later became disillusioned with the party and resigned, but she never abandoned her belief in socialism. She spoke about her views to a reporter for the* Charleston (West Virginia) Gazette *in 1912.*

"I am simply a social revolutionist. I believe in collective ownership of the means of wealth. At this time the natural commodities of this country are cornered in the hands of a few. The man who owns the means of wealth gets the major profit, and the worker, who produces the wealth from the means in the hands of the capitalist, takes what he can get. Sooner or later, and perhaps sooner than we think, evolution and revolution will have accomplished the overturning of the system under which we now live, and the worker will have gained his own. This change will come as a result of education. My life work has been to educate the worker to a sense of the wrongs he has had to suffer, and does suffer—and to stir up the oppressed to a point of getting off their knees and demanding that which I believe to be rightfully theirs."

vailed throughout the union. But for a time a substantial number of other activists and organizers, Mother Jones among them, fought for the union to be more revolutionary in nature. These unionists saw labor problems in the context of a class struggle. Merely winning higher wages for workers was not going to solve the underlying economic and social inequities in the country. In their opinion, change would have to be more fundamental than that.

The socialists believed that labor unions should have a broader social agenda than that which pragmatists had in mind. That agenda would ideally include education for all workers, government ownership of the means of production (which meant that the government, not individuals, would own the factories and mines), and a fundamental restructuring of the socioeconomic system to favor people over profits.

Although she supported socialist ideas throughout her lifetime, Mother Jones herself was not interested in discussing or debating theories. She was usually impatient with theory and eager to put her ideas into practice instead. "She was not a serious student of political theory or economic theory, the way many of the [other organizers] were," writes biographer Linda Atkinson. "She did not take sides in the disputes and soon turned her attention back to the conflicts and problems of the people."[77]

Jones was often described as a doer rather than a thinker, an impression she helped to convey in her speeches. "I have been a Socialist for more than twenty-nine years," she once told a crowd in Seattle, "but I am not one of those who believe that individual freedom is going to drop down from the clouds—while we sleep. The fight can be won, and will be won, but the struggle will be long. . . . I have no patience with those idealists and visionaries who preach fine spun theories. . . . Let us keep our feet on the ground."[78]

## Telling Her Story

Given her preference for action over words, it is not suprising that Mother Jones quickly grew impatient with writing her autobiography, a task she undertook in 1923. Sometime during that year, she traveled to Chicago to work on the project with an editor, Mary Field Parton. Recent evidence indicates that at least part of the autobiography was dictated rather than written. Still, Mother Jones did not enjoy the solitary nature of the project or the slow pace of written work. This frustration shows in the book, where the first sixty years of her life are summed up in just a few short paragraphs. Very few details are offered regarding Jones's personal life and considerable sorrows, much to the disappointment of anyone eager for information about this remarkable woman.

The book plays loose with facts and dates, too. In a typical example, Mother Jones mentions joining a union, the Knights of Labor, on a certain date, but records show that the Knights did not even admit women until years after the date she listed. Jones had a reputation for embellishing her anecdotes at times, and

*After 1922 Jones's health began to fail, and she was finally forced to slow her pace.*

some episodes in the book lack a witness who could verify Jones's account of an incident. Historians agree that the book cannot be entirely trusted, especially regarding dates and other facts. But the autobiography is still considered a most valuable document, in no small part for the way it captures Mother Jones's indomitable spirit.

## Last Days

For a few years after finishing her autobiography, Mother Jones shuttled between

Los Angeles, where the warm weather soothed her rheumatism, and Washington, D.C., where she would stay with Emma Powderly. After 1922, her health began to fail, rheumatism made walking difficult, and she was finally forced to slow down. She settled with Emma Powderly in Washington for a few years. When nursing Jones became hard on Emma, Jones moved to Hyattsville, Maryland, at the invitation of Walter and Lillie May Burgess. Walter Burgess was a retired coal miner who had befriended Mother Jones years earlier.

Her health was now steadily deteriorating. She told a reporter, "I'm not going to get up again. I'm just an old war-horse—ready to go into battle but too worn out to move."[79] Strong willed as ever, though, Mother Jones held on. Her condition wavered. Sometimes she was lucid and wakeful; other times she slipped into unconsciousness. Unable to take food very well, she grew weaker. Her one hundredth birthday, celebrated with great fanfare at the farmhouse, was one of her better days.

Six months later, on November 30, 1930, Mother Jones died.

A memorial service at St. Gabriel's Roman Catholic Church in Washington, D.C., was well attended by high-ranking labor union officials, the secretary of labor, numerous friends, miners, and other working people. That afternoon her casket was placed on a train and transported to Mt. Olive, Illinois, where, according to her wishes, Mother Jones was to be buried in the Union Miners' Cemetery. At a ceremony in Mt. Olive, a young miner eulogized "the sweet old lady" who had paid his parents a visit seven years earlier. "I knew she was a scrapper and I expected to see a tough old person with a hard voice," he remembered. "Instead, I saw an old-fashioned woman, kind of like the old ladies in the movies that sit at home and do embroidery. You couldn't have helped loving her."[80]

The Rev. John McGuire, himself a labor activist, gave a speech that concluded with these stirring words:

---

## Labor's Hall of Fame

*The following quote from the* United Mine Workers Journal, *excerpted from the special issue in the book* Mother Jones Speaks, *praises Jones's spirited nature.*

"'Mother Jones' lived as few humans have dared to, giving of her great heart and courage for the disinherited, accepting in return hardships, danger and the small pay of a union organizer. She was in scores of jails, confined in the 'bull-pen' many times, tried often on charges of accessory to murder and similar 'crimes.' Neither courts, nor gunmen, nor prisons, nor militia could stop her. Her name will stand at the head among the great of labor's hall of fame."

---

Today in gorgeous mahogany-furnished and carefully guarded offices in distant capitols wealthy mine owners and capitalists are breathing sighs of relief. Today upon the plains of Illinois, the hillsides and valleys of Pennsylvania and West Virginia, in California, Colorado and British Columbia, strong men and toil-worn women are weeping tears of bitter grief. The reason for this contrasting relief and sorrow is the same. Mother Jones is dead.[81]

Ten to fifteen thousand people filled the streets around a Catholic church for the funeral the following day. A choir of miners sang the mass. Years earlier, Mother Jones had come to Mt. Olive to celebrate Virden Day, held in honor of four miners brutally murdered in 1898 by company guards in the nearby Virden coal mines. At the time she expressed the wish to be buried one day alongside the "Virden martyrs," so that she might "sleep in the clay beside those brave boys."[82] Her wish was honored.

## An Assessment

Sadly, Mother Jones did not live to see unions take hold in all fifty states, nor to appreciate the sweeping changes in the labor movement that new laws would make possible in just a few years. Big business had grown rapidly in the 1920s, and attacking the labor movement and "union busting" were popular pastimes throughout the decade. Union memberships declined dramatically. Mother Jones was discouraged by these setbacks. When she died in 1930, the U.S. economy was in the grip of the Great Depression. The stock market had crashed a year earlier, more than ten million people were unemployed, and hunger and homelessness were sweeping the land, much as they had in Ireland the year Jones was born.

But these setbacks were temporary. In the years between Mother Jones's birth and death, much had changed for the better for working people. Labor reform was too solidly under way to allow a return to the brutalities of former days. Within a few years of Jones's death, Congress passed the Wagner Act giving workers the right to union representation in every state in the country. Coming years would see further progressive legislation, and developments such as the formation of the National Labor Relations Board. In laying the groundwork for these advances, Mother Jones and the other early organizers had done their jobs well.

The labor movement and its historians have been slow to recognize Mother Jones's significance, however. Although she was present at the initial meeting of the short-lived Industrial Workers of the World (IWW), she is not usually credited with helping to found that union. No institutional monuments are dedicated to her at the Department of Labor, and no mention is made of her in the department's *Brief History of the American Labor Movement*. Mother Jones's name is not likely to be listed in the index of history books unless they are recently published. For decades, her contribution went largely unacknowledged in any official way.

In part, that is because Mother Jones's significance to the labor movement is somewhat hard to measure in standard ways. Unlike such labor figures as John

*Mother Jones, shown here with President Coolidge, will long be remembered as an inspirational leader and a dedicated fighter for workers' rights.*

Mitchell, whom she vehemently opposed, she was not a president of a union or even a high-ranking official. Her lifelong job was the low-status but essential one of convincing workers to join the union. Instead of drafting documents or writing treatises, as leaders often do, she gave speeches, many of which were never recorded and so are unavailable for study. Information about her personal life has always been scarce. She was a woman who worked in a male-dominated environment well before women's rights, a fact that may help explain both her lowly position in the union and the lack of credit she has been given.

Today we recognize the considerable impact Mother Jones had on working people's lives. As a union organizer, she drew great numbers of workers to the ranks of the UMWA. She gave inspiration, encouragement, and moral support to workers and was the driving force behind many successful strikes. She raised money for the union cause, attracted publicity when it was helpful, pushed for numerous congressional investigations, helped innocent people out of prison, and made a difference in countless ordinary lives.

Among working people, Mother Jones has always been much loved. After her death, she attained the legendary status of a folk hero. Songwriters composed ballads about her, artists sketched her likeness, and writers based their works on her. Playwrights, in particular, have found her dramatic life inspiring, and she is the subject of numerous stage plays. Since 1980 there has been a resurgence of interest in her life and work, especially among scholars. And she continues to inspire working people. During the Pittston coal strike of 1989–90, a group of women who call themselves the Daughters of Mother Jones—mostly strikers' wives and relatives—organized to work for change in the spirit of Mother Jones. A popular magazine devoted to investigative journalism is named after her. Her likeness can be found on postcards, T-shirts, and greeting cards. In towns around the country, an increasing number of Mother Jones festivals, dinners, and other events take place in her honor. Mother Jones remains a lively presence even today.

# Notes

### Introduction: Fighting Like Hell for the Living

1. Quoted in Dale Fetherling, *Mother Jones: The Miners' Angel.* Carbondale: Southern Illinois University Press, 1974, p. 8.
2. Quoted in Fetherling, *The Miners' Angel*, p. 10.
3. Quoted in Linda Atkinson, *Mother Jones: The Most Dangerous Woman in America.* New York: Crown, 1978, p. 1.
4. Quoted in Mary Field Parton, ed., *The Autobiography of Mother Jones*, 4th ed., revised. Chicago: Charles H. Kerr, 1990, p. 41.

### Chapter 1: "I Was Born in Revolution"

5. Quoted in Irving Werstein, *Labor's Defiant Lady: The Story of Mother Jones.* New York: Thomas Y. Crowell, 1969, p. 14.
6. Quoted in Werstein, *Labor's Defiant Lady*, p. 16.
7. Quoted in Parton, *Autobiography of Mother Jones*, p. 12.
8. Quoted in Parton, *Autobiography of Mother Jones*, p. 13.

### Chapter 2: An Instinct to Break the Chains

9. Quoted in Parton, *Autobiography of Mother Jones*, p. 14.
10. Quoted in Fetherling, *The Miners' Angel*, p. 11.
11. Werstein, *Labor's Defiant Lady*, p. 41.
12. Quoted in Parton, *Autobiography of Mother Jones*, p. 16.

13. Quoted in Parton, *Autobiography of Mother Jones*, p. 21.
14. Quoted in Parton, *Autobiography of Mother Jones*, p. 22.

### Chapter 3: The Coal Miners

15. Quoted in Atkinson, *Mother Jones*, p. 103.
16. Quoted in Priscilla Long, *Where the Sun Never Shines: A History of America's Bloody Coal Industry.* New York: Paragon, 1989, p. 157.
17. Quoted in Steel, *The Speeches and Writings of Mother Jones*, p. xv.
18. Quoted in Philip S. Foner, ed., *Mother Jones Speaks: Collected Speeches and Writing.* New York: Monad Press, 1983, p. 163.
19. Quoted in Parton, *Autobiography of Mother Jones*, p. 35.
20. Quoted in Parton, *Autobiography of Mother Jones*, p. 37.
21. Quoted in Fetherling, *The Miners' Angel*, p. 30.
22. Quoted in Atkinson, *Mother Jones*, p. 104.
23. Quoted in Atkinson, *Mother Jones*, p. 105.
24. Quoted in Fetherling, *The Miners' Angel*, p. 32.
25. Quoted in Fetherling, *The Miners' Angel*, p. 37.
26. Quoted in Parton, *Autobiography of Mother Jones*, p. 65.
27. Quoted in Parton, *Autobiography of Mother Jones*, p. 69.

### Chapter 4: March of the Mill Children

28. Quoted in Parton, *Autobiography of Mother Jones*, p. 71.

29. Quoted in Atkinson, *Mother Jones*, p. 118.

30. Quoted in Parton, *Autobiography of Mother Jones*, p. 72.

31. Quoted in Atkinson, *Mother Jones*, p. 122.

32. Quoted in Werstein, *Labor's Defiant Lady*, p. 10.

33. Quoted in Atkinson, *Mother Jones*, p. 124.

34. Quoted in Werstein, *Labor's Defiant Lady*, p. 13.

35. Quoted in Werstein, *Labor's Defiant Lady*, p. 14.

36. Quoted in Atkinson, *Mother Jones*, p. 132.

37. Atkinson, *Mother Jones*, p. 133.

### Chapter 5: Warfare in West Virginia

38. Quoted in Parton, *Autobiography of Mother Jones*, p. 1.

39. Edward M. Steel, ed., *The Correspondence of Mother Jones*. Pittsburgh: University of Pittsburgh Press, 1985, p. xxvi.

40. Quoted in Foner, *Mother Jones Speaks* p. 156.

41. Quoted in Atkinson, *Mother Jones*, p. 170.

42. Quoted in Foner, *Mother Jones Speaks*, p. 157.

43. Quoted in Foner, *Mother Jones Speaks*, p. 164.

44. Quoted in Judith Nies, *Seven Women: Portraits from the American Radical Tradition*. New York: Viking, 1977, p. 121.

45. Quoted in Atkinson, *Mother Jones*, p. 3.

46. Quoted in Atkinson, *Mother Jones*, p. 182.

47. Quoted in Foner, *Mother Jones Speaks*, p. 161.

48. Quoted in Atkinson, *Mother Jones*, p. 183.

49. Quoted in Foner, *Mother Jones Speaks*, p. 223.

50. Quoted in Foner, *Mother Jones Speaks*, p. 224.

### Chapter 6: Back to Colorado

51. Quoted in Atkinson, *Mother Jones*, p. 188.

52. Foner, *Mother Jones Speaks*, p. 227.

53. Quoted in Fetherling, *The Miners' Angel*, p. 117.

54. Quoted in Fetherling, *The Miners' Angel*, p. 118.

55. Quoted in Atkinson, *Mother Jones*, p. 194.

56. Quoted in Atkinson, *Mother Jones*, p. 199.

57. Quoted in Parton, *Autobiography of Mother Jones*, p. 185.

58. Quoted in Fetherling, *The Miners' Angel*, p. 124.

59. Quoted in Fetherling, *The Miners' Angel*, p. 124.

60. Quoted in Joan C. Hawxhurst, *Mother Jones: Labor Crusader*. Austin: Raintree Steck-Vaughn, 1994, p. 98.

61. Quoted in Atkinson, *Mother Jones*, p. 203.

62. Quoted in Atkinson, *Mother Jones*, p. 206.

63. Quoted in Fetherling, *The Miners' Angel*, p. 126.

64. Quoted in Fetherling, *The Miners' Angel*, p. 127.

65. Quoted in Fetherling, *The Miners' Angel*, p. 132.

66. Quoted in Fetherling, *The Miners' Angel*, p. 132.

67. Quoted in Fetherling, *The Miners' Angel*, p. 134.

68. Quoted in Fetherling, *The Miners' Angel*, p. 136.

69. Quoted in Parton, *Autobiography of Mother Jones*, p. 202.

### Chapter 7: "The Future Is in Labor's Strong, Rough Hands"

70. Quoted in Parton, *Autobiography of Mother Jones*, p. 213.

71. Quoted in Parton, *Autobiography of Mother Jones*, p. 203.

72. Quoted in Atkinson, *Mother Jones*, p. 227.

73. Atkinson, *Mother Jones*, p. 227.

74. Quoted in Long, *Where the Sun Never Shines*, p. 157.

75. Quoted in Foner, *Mother Jones Speaks*, p. 25.

76. Quoted in Parton, *Autobiography of Mother Jones*, p. 7.

77. Atkinson, *Mother Jones*, p. 159.

78. Quoted in Foner, *Mother Jones Speaks*, p. 249.

79. Quoted in Fetherling, *The Miners' Angel*, p. 201.

80. Quoted in Fetherling, *The Miners' Angel*, p. 208.

81. Quoted in Foner, *Mother Jones Speaks*, p. 67.

82. Quoted in Fetherling, *The Miners' Angel*, p. 207.

# For Further Reading

Linda Atkinson, *Mother Jones: The Most Dangerous Woman in America*. New York: Crown, 1978. A highly readable and informative account intended for readers in grade 6 and above.

Jean Bethell, *Three Cheers for Mother Jones*. New York: Holt, Rinehart & Winston, 1980. A fictionalized account of the march of the mill children. A dramatic and well-written story for young readers.

Joan C. Hawxhurst, *Mother Jones: Labor Crusader*. Austin: Raintree Steck-Vaughn, 1994. A very thorough, well-researched, recent biography of Mother Jones written for junior high readers.

Judith Nies, *Seven Women: Portraits from the American Radical Tradition*. New York: Viking, 1977. Contains a short but engaging chapter on Mother Jones, seen here as one in a line of female activists.

Irving Werstein, *Labor's Defiant Lady: The Story of Mother Jones*. New York: Thomas Y. Crowell, 1969. A fast-moving account of Mother Jones's life, one of the first written for young readers.

# Works Consulted

Dale Fetherling, *Mother Jones: The Miners' Angel*. Carbondale: Southern Illinois University Press, 1974. The most thorough and detailed adult biography of Mother Jones to date.

Philip S. Foner, ed., *Mother Jones Speaks: Collected Speeches and Writing*. New York: Monad Press, 1983. A fascinating collection of Mother Jones's more famous speeches, including articles she wrote for publication in labor-related journals and newspapers. Has a lengthy introduction and notes that provide a context for the speeches, but both contain errors.

Ronnie Gilbert, *Ronnie Gilbert on Mother Jones: Face to Face with the Most Dangerous Woman in America*. Berkeley: Conari Press, 1993. A script for a play in which the author imagines a long conversation with Mother Jones about Jones's life and accomplishments. Suggests new ways to look at Jones's antifeminism. Entertaining and informative, though not to be taken as factual.

Priscilla Long, *Where the Sun Never Shines: A History of America's Bloody Coal Industry*. New York: Paragon, 1989. Useful background reading, especially for historical information on coal mining in the Colorado mountains.

Mary Field Parton, ed., *The Autobiography of Mother Jones*. 4th ed., revised. Chicago: Charles H. Kerr, 1990. Mother Jones's own account of her life. Contains several inaccuracies and some unverifiable anecdotes. A valuable portrait nonetheless.

Edward M. Steel, ed., *The Correspondence of Mother Jones*. Pittsburgh: University of Pittsburgh Press, 1985. A collection of previously unpublished letters written between 1900 and 1930, edited by a well-respected labor historian.

——, *The Speeches and Writings of Mother Jones*. Pittsburgh: University of Pittsburgh Press, 1988. Mother Jones's speeches to miners conventions and her articles from the *Appeal to Reason*, *International Socialist Review*, and other publications. The editor provides a lengthy academic introduction.

U.S. Department of Labor, Bureau of Labor Statistics, *Brief History of the American Labor Movement*. 5th ed., Bulletin 1000. Washington, D.C.: GPO, 1976. A basic overview, written in simple, straightforward style, of the labor movement in America. Helpful background for understanding Mother Jones's career, although she is not mentioned in its pages.

# Index

# Picture Credits

Cover photo: The Bettmann Archive

Archive Photos, 27, 63

The Bettmann Archive, 30, 44, 80

Culver Pictures, Inc., 11, 74

Library of Congress, 10, 13, 15, 16, 18, 19, 22, 25, 28, 32, 34, 35 (both), 36, 41, 42, 45, 47, 48, 50, 53, 57, 58, 62, 64, 65, 68, 69, 70, 71, 72, 75, 77, 83

West Virginia and Regional History Collection, West Virginia University Libraries, 55, 56

# About the Author

Madelyn Horton is a writer who lives in Seattle with her husband and two young sons. She is at work on a doctorate in English at the University of Washington. This is her second book for Lucent Books.